The Northern Spotted Owl

(strix occidentalis caurina)

An Oregon View
1975 - 2002

By:

Benjamin B. Stout

Order this book online at www.trafford.com
or email orders@trafford.com

Most Trafford titles are also available at major online book retailers.

Print information available on the last page.

ISBN: 978-1-5539-5890-1 (sc)

Trafford rev. 01/15/2020

 www.trafford.com
North America & international
toll-free: 1 888 232 4444 (USA & Canada)
fax: 812 355 4082

CONTENTS

ACKNOWLEDGEMENTS

This story of the northern spotted owl and Oregon could not have been written without the material that Rep. Liz VanLeeuwen collected during her tenure in the House of Representatives in the State of Oregon. I thank her and her many staff that dutifully noted on every item saved the name and date of the publisher. I thank them for collecting pieces that reflected the gamut of opinion regarding the owl. The collection is balanced and that is important to note.

Larry Irwin provided the picture of the owl on the cover. I thank Dr. Irwin and NCASI for the picture and especially the quantitative, well designed experiments that are on going in the attempt to understand the biology of the northern spotted owl.

David F. Stout, my son, did yeoman duty in editing the manuscript. I thank him for his efforts. Errors that still remain in either presentation or content are my responsibility.

Elaine H. Stout has been both supportive and tolerant of my single-minded devotion to this project. What started out to be just a few hours effort has gone on for over three years. It has been a labor of love and I thank her for sharing.

Benjamin B. Stout
January 2003

PROLOGUE

Most national forests in the West were established early in the 20th century. The Forest Service in the U. S. Department of Agriculture managed them. Because the forests were removed from the public domain and not subject to local government taxes, payments in lieu of taxes were paid in the counties where the national forests were located. The Bureau of Land Management in the U. S. Department of Interior also managed forestland under its control, and it, too, made payments in lieu of taxes.

There are 27.99 million acres of forestland in Oregon. Seventy seven percent of that area (21.6 million acres) is classified as timberland. That is, land on which commercial timber can be grown. The federal government owns 55 percent of that land. Oregon has at least 2.9 million acres in Wilderness and other areas that have restricted use and timber harvest is not permitted. Much of the 2.9 million acres is so-called old growth forest; how much is hotly debated because an agreement cannot be reached on a single definition for old growth.

There are many laws that govern how federal land shall be managed. The National Forest Management Act (NMFA), the Endangered Species Act (ESA), the National Environmental Policy Act, (NEPA), and the Clean Water Act (CWA) are the major guides for forest management on federal land. The acts are not always in perfect harmony; conflicting guides exist. The conflicting guides are subject to various interpretations, depending on the attitude of mind of the interpreter.

The U. S. Forest Service was primarily a forest custodian during the first half of the 20th Century. After World War II the Forest Service's role expanded and timber was harvested from the national forests at an increasing rate. Concerns were raised during the 1960s and early 1970s about the ways and amounts of timber being harvested. The passage of NMFA in 1976 was Congress' way of addressing the concerns being raised and to broaden the perspective of the Forest Service in its management of the national forests. Even with NMFA in place, which required public involvement in the development of management plans for the forests, earlier concerns were not addressed in the eyes of many. As levels of harvest continued to rise in the 1980s the levels of concern were also raised.

Into this milieu came the ESA. State and local governments had learned to depend on payments in lieu of taxes from the federal government based on the amount of federal timber harvested each year. They were fearful of losing that revenue.

As we shall see, the proponents of reduced or no timber harvest on federal land used the ESA as the focal point for their arguments. The

1

northern spotted owl was the principal species to carry their banner. They hoped for a 90 percent reduction in timber harvest and got nearly 100 percent.

Those who sought continued harvest of timber from the national forests were concerned about jobs, infrastructure, and families in the communities dependent on federal timber for family wage jobs.

As representative of the old 37th House District of Oregon that included a large segment of the Willamette National Forest, Liz VanLeeuwen foresaw serious problems for her constituents if the timber harvests were reduced substantially on federal forests. We shall see that in the 1980s hers was a strident voice for good science. She was a critic of the ESA because her people were not being considered in programs to protect the owl. She fought valiantly. She brought to bear her knowledge of things biological—she is a partner in a successful grass seed farm, a graduate of Oregon State University, and a native Oregonian. Her service in the state legislature, which began in 1981 following a long period of volunteer service of many kinds, had taught her to examine carefully programs being offered on silver platters by government bureaucrats. Despite this the bird was listed, timber harvests were reduced to near zero and many of her constituents suffered.

A collection of material that filled seven large cartons was examined piece by piece and a database of 1300 items was developed. From that database 360 citations are used to indicate the sources of information that under gird the story presented.

What becomes evident as the story unfolds is that the checks and balances on which our system is supposed to function failed. Questions about where and how owl sampling was done, about the range of forest conditions that could support owls, about what is old growth, about the role of federal forests in community stability, about the impact of the ESA on people and communities, about personal biases influencing scientific findings, and about scientific objectivity and academic freedom were widely debated and rarely resolved.

Here is a record of what an intensely interested legislator knew, how she knew it and how she tried to influence the flow of events.

CHAPTER ONE

THE NORTHERN SPOTTED OWL

INTRODUCTION

The northern spotted owl (*Strix occidentalis caurina*) and the Endangered Species Act (ESA) have wrought major changes in the way the forests of the region are used to benefit society.

A bird and a law have combined to influence the Pacific Northwest in many ways. This interaction between a bird and the law took place during the tenure of a state legislator who served a district that encompassed a large segment of the Willamette National Forest and lands managed by the Bureau of Land Management. Many constituents' jobs depended on timber from that federal land, in the woods and in the mills. Representative Liz VanLeeuwen, District 37, diligently saved all the papers that pertained to the owl story. What follows are the gleanings from seven large cartons of material related to the northern spotted owl. The arrangement is essentially chronological. The story begins in the early 1980s. It is still being played out in 2002, and will surely extend well into the 21st century.

The purpose is to assemble in one place a history of the development of the Saga of the Spotted Owl as lived by a legislator who was intensely interested. There were and are many actors. People, communities and local officials, state and federal agencies, politicians and bureaucrats, industries, environmentalists, scientists, and the media all played roles in and influenced the story as it developed.

This is the story of how the idea that the owl is going extinct reduced an industry to shambles to save a bird that now, in hindsight, seems either quite capable of taking care of itself or is being decimated by the barred owl.

EARLY WARNINGS

A graduate student in wildlife biology at Oregon State University, Eric Forsman, chose as his subject species for a graduate degree the northern spotted owl (NSO). It was well known that NSO were few in number and widely distributed in the forests of the Pacific Northwest. The common belief was that NSO lived exclusively in old growth forest. That is where Forsman looked and found NSO.

The mature forest on federal land in the Pacific Northwest was essentially untouched until after World War II. Beginning in the 1950s management of the federal land involved more and more harvest of the wood that had accumulated in these forests since the last major natural disturbance that occurred from 200 to perhaps 650 years ago. The forests on federal land were a mosaic of stands of different ages, all dating from the disturbance that triggered regeneration. In the Douglas-fir region the oldest trees are usually 650 years old or younger. It is approximately 10,000 years since the last advance of the Pleistocene ice. Why not forests 10,000 years old? The answer is disturbance—fire, wind, insects, and disease. These disturbing factors eliminate the forests—the Tillamook fires are classic examples—periodically, usually every 650 years or fewer. We can use the 650-year value to estimate at least how many times the forests have been devastated and regenerated: about 16 times or 10,000 divided by 650.

The harvest of timber from federal land reached a peak in 1988. These are the forests that have been variously labeled as old growth, Ancient Forest, mature forest and each name carries a special connotation. The first two connote forests that have been there "forever." Hence they have a mystical value. The latter suggests a forest that has reached maturity and could be harvested and replaced with a young, vigorous forest.

A map in an early United States Geological Survey report [1] shows surprisingly small areas of really old, that is, 650 years old or older, forest. The disturbance regime is real.

The conventional wisdom was that NSO lived only in mature forests; mature forests on federal land were being cut; therefore the population of the owls must be declining. That being the case, then the ESA needed to be used to prevent the NSO from becoming extinct.

THE ACTORS

Biologists

Wildlife biologists employed by federal and state agencies are featured actors in this drama. The United States Forest Service (USFS), the Bureau of Land Management (BLM), the United States Fish and Wildlife Service (USFWS) and the Oregon Department of Fish and Wildlife (ODFW) are the major employers of these biologists. Forest industry also had wildlife biologists involved.

Attorneys.

Bureaucrats.

Forest industry association employees.

State and federal legislators.

4

The legislators' actions were largely aimed at seeking accommodation for constituents while living within the strictures of ESA.

Media, here being the newspapers of the region, reported on the news and commented in editorials on what was being observed. There is no record in Rep. VanLeeuwen's collection of materials showing television or radio comments.

Environmental organizations sought to achieve their objectives using NSO as a lever. One of the choicest comments by an environmentalist, Andy Stahl, was, "If the spotted owl had not evolved we would have had to invent it to save the forests." [2]

The courts have been major players in the drama. No matter what decision an agency made about managing federal forests, some group would soon disagree with the decision. The courts became the controlling branch of the federal establishment in the management or non-management of federal forestland.

Citizens, either through individual initiative via letters to editors or in organizations, have sought to influence the debate on NSO. In the process they have revealed the depth of despair felt in families and communities impacted by reduced harvest of timber on federal land.

One economist frequently summed up discussions—arguments—with this: "It all comes down to money." Federal law stipulates that a portion of the money USFS and BLM get from timber sales goes to local governing bodies for infrastructure and schools. Congress has provided in-kind payments as timber harvest has declined. So for every local politician or school board member in Oregon, urban or rural, the amount of timber money is an important segment on the income side of a budget.

Ideas make the world go around, so it is said. The actors in this drama all had ideas. Many of the ideas were diametrically opposed. The story at any time had the appearance of a whirling dervish due to the conflicting ideas. We seek an understanding of the impact of all these ideas on the people and the forests of the Pacific Northwest.

CHAPTER TWO

THE OWL— PERSPECTIVES

"The northern spotted owl (*Strix occidentalis caurina*) is one of the most studied and best known owls in the world."[3] This wealth of knowledge has its origins in the work of Eric Forsman and later collaborators. In 1976 Forsman did a master's thesis on the NSO.[4] That was followed by a doctoral dissertation in 1980.[5] That led to the Forsman, et al. paper of 1984.[6] With these, and other related reports the idea that the NSO was in trouble was firmly fixed in the minds of many biologists. Because finding the birds required extensive fieldwork, it became relatively easy to begin using the bird's alleged need for old growth habitat to raise alarms about the species' survival.

During the late 1970s and 1980s the harvest of timber on national forests and BLM land, predominantly old growth, increased dramatically. Therefore, if old growth was being harvested at increased rates, it would seem to follow that a bird associated with old growth—some said dependent on it—would have to be in trouble. For those concerned for all sorts of reasons about the increased timber harvest, it became ever more clear that the NSO and the Endangered Species Act could be used to slow or halt the harvest of timber on federal land.

THE ENVIRONMENTALIST STRATEGY

In a presentation at the sixth annual Western Public Interest Law Conference at the University of Oregon's Law School, in 1988, Andy Stahl, cited above, a resource analyst at the Sierra Legal Defense Fund in Seattle, WA, is reported to have said,

"I'm going to talk about litigation strategies to delay federal timber sales on Bureau of Land Management and Forest Service land which log old-growth forests.

"Until litigation is adopted which protects these forests, we need at least one surrogate, if you will, that will provide protection for these forests. A surrogate must have three qualities to be a good surrogate. First, it must be unique to old-growth forests; secondly, it must be measurable using scientific methods; and third, it must, of course, enjoy some amount of statutory protection.

"Well, as the strategy for protecting old-growth matured, it appeared that wildlife would offer the most fruitful hunting grounds for a surrogate that meets these three criteria. It's quite biologically sensible to hypothesize that one or more species of wildlife would, in fact, be unique to old-growth

6

forest, because such forests were for millennia the dominant forest type in the Pacific Northwest. In addition, wildlife is measurable; you can count them. And, as we'll see, you can count them in amusingly simple ways. And, thanks to the work of Walt Disney with Bambi and her friends…wildlife enjoys substantial, substantive, statutory protection.

"Well, the northern spotted owl is the wildlife species of choice to act as a surrogate for old-growth protection, and I've often thought that thank goodness the spotted owl evolved in the Northwest, for if it hadn't, we'd have to genetically engineer it. It's a perfect species for use as a surrogate."

Mr. Stahl's candid assessment of the situation fixed the real focus of environmentalist concerns: old growth. There were those who did not want the old growth forests cut for any reason. Despite the fact that millions of acres of old growth are reserved in national parks and designated wilderness on national forests, many wanted all old growth preserved. In later years, as we shall see, removing people from the land was a goal also.

The rhetoric used to accomplish this was demonstrated in Mr. Stahl's remarks. He calls "old growth" a forest type, an inaccurate description. Forest types correctly refer to the species of trees that make up that forest; a type can be young or old.

A POLITICIAN

Liz VanLeeuwen, Representative of then District #37 in the Oregon Legislature, wrote in late 1986 about her concerns regarding the management of national forests, particularly the one that formed a large part of her district—the Willamette National Forest. In an op-ed piece discussing impending plans for the Forest she wrote:

"I have reviewed the Forest Service Proposal to designate 1.8 million acres of old-growth timber as habitat for the spotted owl. I feel that the preferred alternative is excessive and premature on the information available.

"I am greatly concerned that the Forest Service plan will eliminate some 4,800 direct and indirect jobs in the region. As far as I can tell, nearly 400 of those jobs will be lost in District 37 alone. To make matters even worse, this study draws conclusions and makes projections despite incomplete and unavailable data identified in the report. The Forest Service appears willing to sacrifice jobs and our economy based on a mass of opinions, estimates and projections.

"I oppose the preferred alternative on the following grounds:

"1. The northern spotted owl is not on the U. S. Fish and Wildlife list of endangered or threatened species. According to the SEIS, earlier estimates of a population of 1,000 to 1,200 pairs of owls in the state (Oregon) were underestimates.

"2. There is no shortage of owl habitat, nor will there be a shortage in the foreseeable future. At the current rate of harvest, there are expected to be 4 million acres of suitable owl habitat remaining at the end of this century.

"3. The study by the Forest Service fails to provide documentation as to the current owl population needs, habitat or viability. It appears that the only intent of the study is to justify an arbitrary position rather than meet real needs.

"Rather than create an employment or economic crisis in our community over a faulted study, I would rather see the Forest Service adopt a new plan that would give equal weight to our economic stability concerns as to owl habitat preference. I support a plan by the Northwest Forest Resource Council that would provide an extensive research program over the next decade to identify true habitat needs of the owl and to develop a reasonable management plan."[7]

The representative touches on an issue that we will see throughout this saga: the quality and objectivity of scientific research on which policies are based. Another theme will also recur with regularity: the effect natural resource policies have on the lives of Oregonians, particularly those who live in rural areas.

THE PRESS

The Lebanon Express, the local paper in a truly timber dependent community, commented editorially about the NSO decision by the Forest Service.

"Linn County residents concerned with their future, their children's future and the future of essential community services like schools, police protection, fire protection, medical care and transportation networks, should not overlook the importance of the U. S. Forest Service decision concerning the spotted owl.

"At this point the forest service's preferred alternative will set aside 2,200 acres of old growth timber for each of 550 pairs of owls. That's 1.2 million acres. Because of where some of that timber is located, approximately 1.8 million acres will be totally affected. However, some of that timber is already set-aside for other purposes.

"The important number to remember is 690,000—690,000 acres currently managed for timber production that will be taken out of production because of the spotted owls. That's enough to fuel 80 mills for 10 years or 10 mills in perpetuity (considering an 80-year rotation cycle).

"Those 690,000 acres contain 40 billion feet of old growth timber worth $6 billion in Oregon and Washington. Those 690,000 acres will reduce employment by 1,300 workers in the timber industry, and 3,500 more workers in services and associate trades. If this doesn't get the alarms going off in your head, nothing will. Also, $33 million will be eliminated from the federal treasury each year, and county revenues will be cut by $9 million each year.

"The situation is absurd. If the forest service and the environmental groups weren't so serious about this proposal, we wouldn't have believed that this proposal could have gotten this far if you would have described this scenario to us 10 years ago.

"How did the forest service arrive at 2,200 acres per pair of owls? It based its decision on a single, one-year study that tracked the range of only six pairs of owls."[8]

The sentiment in Oregon District 37 strongly favored the needs of people over those owls. As plans by the Forest Service were being developed, local press joined in expressing that sentiment. On July 31, 1986 the Albany *Democrat Herald* had this to say:

"The spotted owl is fast becoming a symbol for preservation of the remaining stands of old-growth timber in the national forests of western Oregon. That may be unfortunate for the spotted owl.

"Depending on how much forest is set aside to accommodate the spotted owl, a smaller or larger number of people in Oregon may lose their jobs in the wood-products industry over the next several years. These may well be people with families to support. When their jobs disappear, they may or may not find other work. Chances are some of them will find it impossible to retrain for something else. Once unemployment runs out and life gets tight, those families will be in a world of hurt.

"We know that persistent joblessness leads to various related problems: Families break up; lives are ruined; even child abuse may increase.

"Forced to choose between accommodating a bird that most people have never seen and forcing joblessness and other problems on your neighbors, most voters in this part of Oregon may just say to heck with the bird. (They would say this if they got a chance to vote on the issue, which they won't.)"[9]

The editorial goes on to discuss the ideas being tossed around for saving the owl and concludes by saying,

"Every reasonable person is in favor of conservation and against destroying nature needlessly or recklessly. Nobody wishes harm on the hapless spotted owl.

"But when it comes to choosing between the survival of Oregon workers and their families on the one hand and the survival of a few hundred owls on the other, we have little choice but to come down on the side of the people, and let the owls fend for themselves."[7]

What seems a reasonable premise to many turns out to be unreasonable from the standpoint of the Endangered Species Act and the findings of federal bureaucrats and biologists in carrying out the Act.

Individuals felt strongly about the dichotomy of owls and jobs. In a letter to the editor Rintha Renoud of Foster had this to say,

"Once again, we have the dubious pleasure of receiving yet another questionable environmental impact statement (EIS).

"The Spotted Owl EIS became available on Aug. 7. With this latest request, Oregon's future is again under siege from the jolly green bigots wishing to create a statewide national park and, in my opinion, a monument to waste and stupidity.

"The EIS process must produce a judicially sustainable document. We must recognize that NEPA (National Environmental Policy Act) is no longer a decision-making tool, but a procedure for court contest. Adequacy and accuracy of documents on all counts is therefore crucial.

"As you review the recommendation for 2,200 acres per pair of spotted owls, please consider the following points for accuracy in your final position. All of the NEPA requirements for an EIS may have been considered, but I question whether the accuracy criteria have been met.

"Facts:

"0   Oregon currently has 2.078 million acres retired permanently to wilderness; 538,774 acres are protected by scenic, national park and other designations. An inventory of this acreage will show that much suitable habitat already exists.

"0 There is no documented, valid research which affirms the premise that old growth stands are the only suitable habitat.

"0 To date no valid inventory of the spotted owl exists.

"0 Withdrawal of the recommended acreage will remove 7 billion board feet of timber (base) from the Willamette National Forest alone.

"0 Further loss of timber base will result in direct and indirect loss of jobs, services reliant on the timber industry, and tax-supported services.

"0 Spotted owls do live and thrive in habitat other than old growth.

Industry. "Living in the state of Oregon is synonymous with 'environmental concern;' it is indeed a household phrase. Involvement inside or outside the timber industry is not a criterion for being a concerned citizen of this state.

"In our zealous rush to offer ever-more protections to the environmental ecosystems, we have ignored one very real ecosystem, the human one. It is not enough to have the simple privilege to live in this state. We must now give equal weight to the privilege of being able to earn a living.

"If this latest 'compromise' from the absurd to the merely ridiculous is adopted, we will certainly see the state of Oregon fall from grace as a strong competitive and genuinely protective leader in the timber industry.

"Oregon's present and Oregon's future are sitting on the railroad tracks, and the train is definitely within sight. Please consider the most basic facts in your deliberation on this issue. This is not an either-or bargain; we can have both if common sense will prevail."[10]

The foregoing is a small part of a much larger outpouring of ideas and sentiment regarding the NSO. The stimulus for this outpouring was action by federal agencies in their effort to comply with existing law regarding land management, including the animal species thereon. The way the national forests were to be managed by the Forest Service was described in a Record of Decision, Final Environmental Impact Statement, issued in March 1992. Therein one finds a succinct recital of the actions leading to the decision:

"The Forest Service previously promulgated management guidelines for the northern spotted owl in the Pacific Southwest Regional Guide in 1984 and in an amendment to the Pacific Northwest Regional Guide in 1988. In October 1989, an Interagency Scientific Committee was established under an interagency agreement among the Forest Service in the U. S. Department of Agriculture, the Bureau of Land Management, and the National Park Service in the U. S. Department of the Interior. This Committee of Scientists was charged with developing a scientifically credible conservation strategy for the northern spotted owl. In its April 1990 report, the Interagency Scientific Committee reported that the spotted owl was imperiled over significant portions of its range and proposed a Conservation Strategy.

"In June 1990, the U. S. Fish and Wildlife Service listed the northern spotted owl as a threatened subspecies throughout its range under the Endangered Species Act."[11]

From the first rumblings about the owl to the listing, all sorts of ideas and purported facts were floating in the air. We turn now to see how some of these ideas were expressed. We will do this in chronological order.

CHAPTER THREE

PEOPLE, OWL, AND COSTS

A wildlife biology graduate student picked a species for a thesis in the mid 1970's. The wheels of federal agencies continued to grind out reports and plans. Decisions were made. Federal laws required that a species that is a part of a forest ecosystem must be accommodated. The Forest Service developed plans to protect the NSO and do the other things called for in managing the national forests. Would there be a cost? Probably!

By the spring of 1986 members of Congress were concerned about how old-growth forests should be managed. The general pattern of management of federal forests then was to increase the harvest of old growth in the Pacific Northwest. Congressional hearings were held. At a hearing of the House of Representatives' Subcommittee on General Oversight, Northwest Power and Forest Management of the Committee on Interior and Insular Affairs, Rep. Van Leeuwen testified.

"My name is Liz VanLeeuwen and I am State Representative for District #37. My district includes Lebanon and Sweet Home and most of western Linn County. I am here today, Rep. Weaver, because I also have concerns about federal management of old growth, as do my constituents.

"According to preliminary March figures from the State Employment Division, some 5,534 Linn County Residents derive their employment directly from the wood and paper products industry. Their future is tied to the wise use of old growth stands in Linn County, particularly those in the Willamette National Forest. Last year, sales of old growth timber from the Forest made up 24.6% of total Linn County tax revenues. So all of us in Linn County benefit directly or indirectly from the harvest of old growth.

"To hear the news reports of the last few weeks, one would think that old growth is an endangered species. On the contrary, over half of the Willamette National Forest is still in old growth and nearly half of that is preserved forever in some kind of congressional or administrative set-aside that prohibits forest management and logging. Old growth is not an endangered species. But our Linn County communities are endangered if those who wish to preserve vast areas of old growth have their way.

"Preliminary estimates from the Forest Service show that the allowable cut on the Willamette National Forest will be reduced 22-30% or more by the forest planning process. This is without additional set-asides such as the Three Creeks Task Force proposal.

"At the end of last year, the Employment Service estimated unemployment in Lebanon at 17% and unemployment in Sweet Home at 20%. Reductions in the harvest of old growth would cause even more serious economic dislocations in these communities.

"We have saved huge segments of the forest for future generations, about one acre per man, woman and child. But you can't put living trees in a museum, expecting them to be exempt from the ravages of nature. You can however, harvest them, replant and manage them wisely to provide beauty, recreation and jobs forever. We need to get on with the business of wisely using and managing the magnificent resource that God gave us."[12]

The early 1980s was a low period for the forest products industry. By 1986 things were looking up. Interest rates were going down and home construction was picking up. Logs from national forests could provide the wood to make the lumber to build the houses. Simultaneously, concerns were being raised about things like the spotted owl. And spotted owls needed big, old trees according to conventional wisdom. Into this situation came an incident that focused the issues in a very pointed way—a major forest industry harvested some old growth on national forest land.

A furor resulted and the difficulty of making wise decisions, even if one knew what was wise, was clearly evident. Into the maelstrom came the Oregon Business Magazine with an editorial lambasting the company for cutting the old growth. The editor, Robert L. Hill, raised the public relations issue. He wrote, rhetorically, "We thought, in a state where the timber industry relies on public lands for the major portion of its raw material, the industry long ago would have learned the importance of good public relations, of having public opinion behind it. Apparently we were wrong. Take Willamette Industries, for instance. To paraphrase a well-known comedian, please take Willamette Industries."

Mr. Hill went on to say:

"Just when interest rates have dropped to the point where a housing boom is being sparked—with all the attendant benefits for this state's timber industry and the overall economy—the industry has to worry that its recovery will be aborted by new forest plans being prepared by the U. S. Forest Service. Those plans will delineate how much timber will be cut every year in national forests and how much will be saved permanently for other recreational uses and to preserve wildlife habitat. Preliminary indications are that those plans, as currently written, will drastically reduce the allowable timber cut on federal lands, in particular the harvest of old-growth timber.

"If that happens, the result could well be more economic problems and unemployment for this state. To combat that possibility, the industry and top public officials are attempting to marshal political allies and rally public opinion in the Northwest to change those plans.

"Then along comes Willamette Industries, and cuts down trees said to be the oldest in the state. In one fell swoop that company did as much for the public image of the timber industry in Oregon as My Lai did for the image of the U. S. Army.

"A lot of people all over Oregon and particularly in the Portland area seldom pay any attention to the timber industry. Now they are talking about the cutting of those trees, and they are mad about it. Those people may not know the difference between a green chain and a tire chain, but they do vote and they contribute to, and influence, politicians, the people who run the Forest Service. We now even have protesters camping out on the lawn of the Federal Building in Eugene to protest the cutting down of the trees.

"In short, the radical environmental movement has been handed a club to hit the entire industry over the head, a club fashioned out of 700-year-old trees cut by Willamette Industries—a company previously known as a good corporate citizen.

"William Shields, a top official of Willamette, spoke before the fifth annual Business Reporting Conference held recently in Salem. He pointed out that the 700- to 1,000-year-old trees were not in a "pristine grove" like the redwoods. The old trees were scattered here and there among much younger trees. Also, the Forest Service allowed the cut after a lengthy legal process even though it knew the age of the trees, Shields said.

"That, quite simply, is not the point. At a time when the timber industry needs all the public support it can get to fight additional bureaucratic controls, at a time when many non-timber-related businesses, this magazine included, want to see the industry succeed in that move, one of the timber kingpins gives the entire industry a black eye.

"What is worse, when Shields was asked by a reporter what Willamette would do if confronted with the same type of situation again, he said the company would do the same thing. That's rule number two of poor public relations—never admit you made a stupid mistake even though everyone knows it.

"This line of thinking will not do. The industry had better get its act together. Public opinion cannot be ignored if the industry wants to continue its harvest of public timber supplies. More importantly, good public relations doesn't just mean issuing press releases and giving speeches; it also involves listening to each other—and thinking."[13]

Mr. Hill's lecture on public relations may have been heard by those outside the business community. One of the many environmental groups active in the mid 1980s was called Cathedral Forest. Their objective was to halt old-growth harvest in the Willamette National Forest east of Sweet Home. On Memorial Day, 1986, Cathedral Forest organized a weekend protest. They arranged for an appearance of jazz artist Paul Winter, who performed what he called "Song of the Cathedral Forest." Winter played a tape recording of the calls of the male and female spotted owl, and then his five-piece group weaved oboe, flute, guitar and drum music into the call. Winter said that he has done similar recordings with the sounds of whales and wolves. Incorporating animal songs and calls into music is his way of giving voice to creatures otherwise left out of natural resources debates.[14]

By mid-1986 stories of the impact of the new forest plans on Oregon were common. Headlines included: "Owl plan would cut Northwest timber harvest"[15], "Spotted owl to cost jobs, increase taxes in Linn"[16] and "F. S. proposal would protect spotted owl."[17]

At the time major changes were underway in the communities that depended on federal timber. What the impact would be was not immediately obvious.

The Sweet Home Ranger District, Willamette National Forest, is in Representative VanLeeuwen's district. Ranger Leonard Lucero, Sweet Home District, reported that while the maximum allowable cut on his district might be reduced, and the actual harvests were not expected to decrease.[18]

The Forest Service planning process produced several alternatives for managing the national forests. The preferred alternative called for providing 550 NSO habitat areas. Each area would be 2,200 acres in extent. The total set aside for NSO protection had various estimates, up to 1.8 million acres, of which up to nearly 700,000 acres were in the land considered suitable for timber production.

When the alternatives were publicized there was immediate reaction. Those concerned with the well-being of the NSO argued for halting timber harvest in all potential owl habitat. Those concerned with the well being of the people, communities and industries argued against removing more land from the timber base.

The Forest Service was flooded with letters of comment on its management plan. It was reported that up to 30,000 letters commenting on the plan were expected.[19] In the same article it was reported that the Forest Service estimated that the preferred alternative would result in the loss of 1300 jobs, and timber revenues shared with counties in Washington and Oregon would drop by $28 to $32 million per year.

Representative VanLeeuwen contributed to the deluge of letters to the Forest Service. On November 5, 1986 she wrote to the regional forester and expressed her opinion that the preferred alternative was excessive and premature based on the information available. In that letter she laid out her reasons for reaching that conclusion:

"I oppose the preferred alternative on the following grounds:

"1. The Northern Spotted Owl is not on the U. S. Fish and Wildlife list of endangered or threatened species. According to the SEIS, 'earlier estimates of a population of 1,000 to 1,200 pairs of owls in the state (Oregon) were underestimated.'

"2. There is no shortage of owl habitat, nor will there be a shortage in the foreseeable future. At the current rate of harvest, there are expected to be 4 million acres of suitable owl habitat remaining at the end of this century.

"3. The study by the Forest Service fails to provide documentation as to the current owl population needs, habitat or viability. It appears that the only intent of the study is to justify an arbitrary position rather than meet real needs."[20]

Representative VanLeeuwen went on to say, "I do not support any reduction in timber sale levels now on behalf of the owl...I urge the Forest Service to adopt a study plan over the next ten to fifteen years that will adequately provide for timber production and our wildlife."

The Albany *Democrat Herald* reported that the Secretary of the Interior, Donald Hodel, was minimizing the impact of old growth harvest on the NSO.[21] Hodel was in Roseburg, OR to support the candidacy of a Republican who was running against Democrat Peter DeFazio to occupy the seat of Congressman Jim Weaver, who was stepping down.

A group calling itself Oregon Resource Equity sent a memorandum to "Parties Interested in Land Management Issues" and shared its interpretation of the NSO issue.[22] Dietz and McCulley pointed out that the Forest Service was proposing to set aside 2,200 acres of old growth for 550 pairs of owls. They give estimates of the value of the timber on those acres—40 billion board feet worth $6 billion, or on a per pair basis, $10 million. They go on to report that the science to support the set aside is not strong, that no one really knows the total population of the owls or of their actual needs for that much additional old growth.

Oregon's senior senator, Mark Hatfield, was involved. In a speech to a planning seminar of the American Bar Association[23] the senator said that the Forest Service should prove that each pair of spotted owls needs 2,200 acres of old-growth fir trees for the species to survive. He asked whether the agency would make balanced decisions on its forest plans for 1987. "The balance is not a set of plans that provide a reduction of 20 percent in timber harvest without biological evidence," Hatfield said. "I haven't seen it (the evidence) and I don't expect to see it."

The news article goes on to say that the Forest Service thinks that Hatfield and other politicians are being misled by the timber industry. New timber sale goals may be 20 percent less than potential yields of forests, but will not differ greatly from actual volumes offer[ed] for sale in the past decade, the agency says.

Industry got involved directly in addition to its support of industry associations. Willamette Industries hired a public relations firm to provide its view of the NSO issue. The Sweet Home, OR *The New Era* reported that the PR firm's assessment of the situation was, "This is not a jobs versus owl issue, it is a jobs versus inadequate information issue. The Forest Service report is filled with too many loopholes, too many questions. The Forest Service officials admit they had limited time to put this report (the EIS) together and they had to work fast to get it out by August..." The PR firm said, "We have undertaken a public awareness program to inform the people of Linn County about the preferred alternative presented by the Forest Service," a representative of the PR firm said. He went on to say that there is no evidence that the owls are endangered at this time.[24]

The Sweet Home Chamber of Commerce captured the essence of community concerns with a resolution:

"WHEREAS, The Sweet Home Chamber of Commerce is concerned with the economic and social well being of the people of Linn County, as well as the future of all species, including the spotted owl, and,

"WHEREAS, Our community is significantly dependent upon a sustained yield of timber from National Forests to provide the base for employment, incomes, and financial support for schools and roads, and,

"WHEREAS, the spotted owl is not federally listed as Threatened or Endangered; and there is a major lack of scientific information on the habitat needs of the species, and,

"WHEREAS, There are about 4.7 million acres of suitable habitat now available to the bird, of which over 4 million acres will remain at the end of the century,

"LET IT THEREFORE BE RESOLVED, The Sweet Home Chamber of Commerce goes on record in opposition to the Forest Service Proposal.

"Respectfully submitted on behalf of the Sweet Home Chamber of Commerce, this 17th day of October, 1986."[25]

The essence of the issue of the NSO and its political inter-weaving was captured in a Letter to the Editor in the fall of 1986:

"I am a housewife with three kids to raise. My husband owns his own small business—auto repair—and he relies on loggers and millworkers for a lot of his business.

"All this fuss about saving the spotted owl, I think, has hidden the real endangered species—the great Oregon working man and woman.

"Peter DeFazio makes a lot of noises about being for the working man, but I think it is all political. Somebody must have told him Democrats are for the working man, but someone else told him Democrats are for the environmentalists. Well, all of us who live in timber towns are environmentalists, but we have no kinship with those radicals who want to stop all logging. And DeFazio is endorsed by those guys. In the Sweet Home area alone they would have locked up 60,000 or more acres in Weaver's wilderness bill, and about five times as much as was finally included in Hatfield's bill.

"Now DeFazio's buddies are trying to put us out of work again by forcing the loggers out of thousands of more acres set aside for the spotted owl. I've got nothing against the spotted owl, but when they're talking about feeding the bird caviar and the loggers beans, then somebody with some reason has to help us.

"Bruce Long, the Republican candidate for Congress, sounds to me like he has some reason. He understands that it takes trees to run sawmills and people with jobs to buy—and repair—cars. We all need each other to give a community or a district a healthy economy, and I think Bruce understands that. It is obvious that his opponent doesn't."[26]

The actions and reactions of people, politicians, industries, interest groups, and federal agencies resembled a cauldron heated to the boiling point and being stirred constantly. The branch of government that really controlled the heat under the cauldron is the judiciary. In the NSO pot the heat was turned up or down—depending on your point of view—in a specific case near Eugene. The news article was an early example of the sort of thing that would happen with federal land management issues in the years to come. In the 1986 article we see the various forces at work.

"PORTLAND (AP)—A federal judge has temporarily blocked logging of two stands of old-growth timber near Eugene pending trial on environmentalists' claims that fish and wildlife habitats would be destroyed.

"Logging on the two areas, which comprise nearly 300 acres 35 miles southeast of Eugene, was to begin on Sept. 29 and Oct. 1.

"Lawyers for two companies holding logging contracts on the areas told U. S. District Judge Edward Leavy in a hearing Friday they would lose money if the harvests were halted.

"Leavy scheduled a trial for Oct. 1 on a lawsuit filed by the Citizens Task Force on Timber Sale Review, which claims that U. S. Forest Service failed to adequately assess the environmental impact of logging the trees.

"The group claims that one of the sites is home to a pair of northern spotted owls, which they say is a threatened species in Oregon.

"Deer and elk also would be jeopardized, as well as populations of cutthroat trout and steelhead, the group contends.

"Defendants in the suit are the Forest Service; its regional forester, James Torrence; Bohemia Inc., which holds the contract on the Duck Soup timber sale; and Zip-O Timber Co. Inc., which holds the contract on the Sad Traverse timber sale.

"Assistant U. S. Attorney Thomas Lee told Leavy the areas were 'exhaustively studied' for the creation of the Willamette National Forest plan, which allocated the areas for logging in 1977.

"Lee said there was a northern spotted owl management area nearby, which the Forest Service considered before deciding to go ahead with the sales.

"Bohemia's lawyer, John Neupert, pointed to the sagging economy in Lane County and told Leavy that any harm the logging caused to the habitat would be 'nothing compared to the harm on these companies if the sales don't go through.'"[27]

CHAPTER FOUR

LULL BEFORE THE STORM
1987-1988

Early 1987 was a quiet time in the natural resource management debate. The Forest Service was busy going through the 41,000 comments regarding the Draft Supplement to the Regional Guide for managing spotted owl habitat. The Draft Supplement had laid out 12 alternatives, A-L, with Alternative F being the preferred alternative. Alternative A was a continuation of existing policy and Alternative L offered the most protection for old growth forest. The preferred alternative satisfied practically no one. The Planning Report[28] shows that 65 percent of the 41,000 respondents commented on the Preferred Alternative and that 99 percent of the comments expressed disapproval. Alternative L received the most support from the public according to the Planning Report; the extent of that support is not given, however.

The Planning Report also includes information, some of which was new, on the spotted owl. It concluded with a section called "Facts about the Spotted Owl." One interesting fact was that forests that had been burned or clearcut within the past 20 years were not used for foraging by the owls; nothing is mentioned about the forests between that age and the older forests, for which the owls seem to have an affinity. The report concludes with this summary: "We cannot say with absolute certainty what kind of habitat the spotted owl needs in order to survive. We do know that it has a strong affinity for the older forests of the Pacific Northwest; that it is more likely to be found roosting, foraging, and nesting in these stands. In developing the Final Supplement, every effort will be made to use the best information on the environmental, social, and economic aspects related to the issue of habitat management for the spotted owl." It would be nearly five years before the final report on the strategy for managing the spotted owl was released.[29]

Finger pointing and sarcastic comments continued during 1987. Richard T. Brown, a resource specialist for the National Wildlife Federation's Pacific Northwest Resources Center in Portland, OR, had this to say:

"For years, conservationists in the Pacific Northwest have warned of the excessive rate of timber cutting on National Forest lands. Not only was logging destroying wildlife and fish habitat, water quality, scenery and recreational opportunities, but it also seemed to exceed a sustainable yield of timber.

"Contrary to Forest Service claims, 'good timber management' did not equate with good habitat management or good watershed management, and projections of future timber growth seemed overly optimistic. Privately, many Forest Service employees (at least those who had to plan timber sales 'on the ground') echoed these concerns.

"There are a number of reasons for optimistic projections of timber productivity. Many of the foresters in charge of the Forest Service came into the agency during the 1950s and 60s, riding the crest of the post-war housing boom and a generally optimistic 'can do' attitude.

"Their training in forestry school followed the European tradition that identified timber as the primary resource of the forest, and intensive forest management was assumed to benefit not only society's desire for wood products, but also watersheds and wildlife. Add incomplete inventories, the traditional bureaucratic imperative to increase one's budget, and a Congress particularly inclined to fund timber programs, and the stage was clearly set for optimistic projections of timber growth and yield.

"The National Forest Management Act of 1976, with its mandate for integrated resource management plans (forest plans), offered some hope that the new inventories and plans would bring timber cutting levels in line with the land's true ability to provide a perpetual supply of timber and the other multiple use resources of the forest. As the national forest planning process has progressed in recent years, it has become clear that there are several things about trees that the Forest Service has inaccurately estimated in the past—how many trees there are, how fast they grow, and, once cut, where they can be grown again.

"In more technical jargon, these estimates are expressed as timber inventories, yield tables and timber land suitability. The pattern of past estimates seems to rather consistently follow the example of the Deschutes National Forest in Oregon, where it was recently revealed that previous estimates of ponderosa pine were 64 % too high.

"Unfortunately these old predictions, speculative as they were, have become the established standard. New, lower, more scientifically based (though still optimistic) calculations are suspect because they run counter to the status quo, and present political, economic and bureaucratic problems.

"As the evidence has accumulated, however, even the Forest Service has felt compelled to request smaller timber budgets in recent years, in an attempt to bring cutting levels more in line with sustained yield and multiple use. What ultimately drives Forest Service programs, however, is what Congress appropriates. While the timber industry successfully maneuvers to delay the issuance of new forest plans, Congress chooses to ignore the new data and funds a timber program consistent with the old, outdated plans.

"These old plans called for a total annual allowable cut level in the Pacific Northwest Region (R-6) of 5.2 billion board feet (bbf). (This is slightly less than half of all the timber cut on all National Forests, and is the equivalent of more than 1 million log truck loads, or more than 5000 clearcuts of 20 acres each.) Conservationists and the timber industry agree that the new plans (if they are ever implemented) would provide for a total of about 4.0 bbf. (And any conservationist in the business will tell you that the new forest plans would still cut most of the roadless areas and old growth, and are not especially sensitive to riparian areas, watersheds, or trails.) Thus, the current timber sale level is at least 30 percent above an optimistic but more nearly sustainable yield of timber, wildlife, water and recreation.

"Historically, silvicultural and economic considerations have caused the oldest stands to be cut first, an approach that has caused the decimation of the Northwest's old growth forests. Though these forests have been seriously depleted, the majority of timber still comes from old growth forests. These majestic forests provide not only essential habitat for many species of wildlife, but evidence mounts that they also provide the key to long-term forest productivity, and consequently economic health and stability.

"The intricate relationships among decaying wood, fungi, wildlife and nutrients for growing trees suggest that we deplete these forests at our peril. Or, one might more accurately say, at the peril of future generations, for they are the ones who will most suffer the consequences of our shortsighted economic and political systems. The extinction of wildlife and loss of water quality may occur in our lifetimes—the failure of trees to grow will come in the future." [30]

There is no doubt that much of what Mr. Brown says is true. There was a period of over cutting in the 1980s brought about by both Congressional and Administration interests. But to end up suggesting that cutting old growth forests perils future generations seems a stretch. For example, European civilization has lived without old growth for centuries. As we have seen earlier, these forests have been taken down numerous times and have regrown following catastrophe. We have no evidence that shows that forests do not regrow. It may take longer than we would prefer, but it does happen. Primary and secondary succession are the processes by which it happens.

Owls are few and far between. They have an "affinity" for old growth. Therefore, how does one deal with owls that are in young forests? One lumberman uses this question to argue the case for continued timber harvest.[31] Bruce L. Engel reports that his company is about to log around the nest of a pair of spotted owls in the Rogue River National Forest. Mr. Engel notes that environmentalists and the Forest Service cared little about the operation. From that he argues that because the owls are using second growth forests for nesting it follows that saving all the old growth may not be crucial after all to save the owl.

With conflicting evidence about the foraging, nesting and resting habitat requirements of the owl and the forest structure needed to meet those requirements it is instructive to look at a 1987 Status Review for the Northern Spotted Owl.[32]

We have seen earlier that concern was expressed over the quality of the science that supported the idea that the northern spotted owl was on its way to extinction. The Status Review puts the knowledge about the NSO in full view. The document ran to 36 pages excluding literature citations and appendices. (The English language uses the subjunctive mood of a verb to convey a sense of possibility rather than an actual fact. Some examples are italicized in what follows.)

Three subspecies of the spotted owl are currently recognized. The subspecific divisions are based on differences in color of plumage. The NSO is the northernmost subspecies with the California subspecies the next one to the south, with the Mexican one the southernmost subspecies. The boundaries between the subspecies are not distinct.[33]

The NSO occurs throughout the coastal mountains in Oregon, as well as the Cascade Range and the Klamath Mountains. Intensive inventories have not been made east of the Cascade crest, though the owl is found east of the Cascades in Washington.[34] Spotted owls *usually* (emphasis added) do not nest every year nor are nesting pairs successful every year.[35] Long-term data necessary to determine trends are lacking on the demography of spotted owls. Reproduction by spotted owls has fluctuated dramatically from year-to-year in some areas. In some years most pairs *may* (emphasis added) breed, whereas in other years very few pairs attempt to nest. Further, it is reported, that it is not clear what influences breeding success and it is unknown if the reproductive fluctuations follow a predictable pattern. Food supply *may* (emphasis added) be the reason for the variation in reproductive activity. East to west differences have been reported and it has been suggested that fluctuations in reproduction and numbers of pairs breeding *may* (emphasis added) be related to fluctuations in prey availability.[36]

The age at which owls start breeding is not known with certainty. Some researchers have *assumed* (emphasis added) it begins at age two and others have assumed age three.[37] Owls are territorial[38] and this generates problems in counting. Only those adults that have established a territory will defend it, and owls are counted by using calls, which mimic another owl and generate a response from the territorial owl. So, a single owl may or may not respond to a call.

To the interested citizen, the Status Review is an exercise in frustration. We are dealing with a bird that apparently never had high population levels, that is hard to pin down from the standpoint of basic biology, and which has competition from other birds. Great horned owls, goshawks, and Coopers hawks are possible predators. The barred owl may displace the NSO.[39] With so many *mays* and *appears* it is not immediately obvious how final conclusions about owl populations can be drawn. Nevertheless, the bureaucracy moved ahead with efforts to protect the NSO from extinction. The impact of this effort on private citizens was reflected in a poem by Gordon Ross, a commissioner in Coos County, OR, which is a take-off on the Rhyme of the Ancient Mariner.

Rhyme of the Ancient Forester
(Or Timber, Timber Everywhere and not a Tree to Cut)

There was an ancient Forester
and he went to fell his tree.
With thy court injunctions
and endless appeals
Why stoppest thou now me?

This land was set aside my friend
to grow this very tree.
Was saved from other uses
For this very one you see.

This land was zoned for resource
by the county and the state.
It was saved for growing timber
lest development be its fate.

The process was judicial
and received the state's own seal.
Now we thought it was our own land
but it survived every appeal.

So we planted it and watered it.
Drove forty-mile round trip.
Did our precommercial thinning
Followed every forest tip.

Fought the moth and then the beetle
and the mountain boomer too.
Cost 200 bucks an acre
but we pulled the whole crop through.

Now we've finally got em grown,
watched the market rise and fall.
Thought we'd harvest and retire
'fore the grim reaper's shroud and pall.

But the bureaucrats been worken
while we were plantin trees.
Got some more considerations
Just a few now if you please.

We'd figured on the streambanks
for a hundred feet or so
We'd have to leave it uncut
just to shade or block the flow.

And a snag or two we'd planned
to leave for the cavity dwellers.
And a live tree here and there
for some other kind a fellers.

What we didn't figure on was
no forty percent cover
With another forty percent
with trees just tuchen one another.

With at least two hundred species
need'n every bit as such
It come to the place now
where Ma and Pa don't count for much.

Now this whole thing is for the birds
and I don't know who's to blame.
But if you don't wear feathers,
You just haven't any claim.

So I dreamed the other night,
that I was hatched instead a born.
And a sadder and a wiser man
I woke the morrow morn.

Concerns about the future were to be found on several fronts. In February 1988 a trio of economists from the Forest Service and University of Minnesota investigated the long-term impacts on the economy of Oregon of alternative timber supply forecasts.[40] They reviewed the history of timber and other jobs in Oregon, and reviewed the history of timber harvesting on private and federal land in southwest Washington after WW II. They reported that the Cooperative Sustained Yield Act of 1944 allowed federal and private land to be managed in concert to prevent a collapse of the timber industry in that region. They suggested that because the law is still on the books it would be wise for a similar arrangement in Oregon in the 1980s. They go on to say:

"Unlike the political scene in 1944, local issues regarding the management of national forests are no longer preeminent. National concerns regarding the preservation of wilderness areas, endangered species, and environmental quality in general has greatly complicated the forest management process...

"One could conjecture that, figuratively speaking, nonmetropolitan Oregon is being colonized by outsiders who exact tribute in the form of environmental imperatives. In any event, there appears to be little likelihood that future public timber harvesting policies will be influenced solely by local concerns." [13]

Economists are often chided for being less than adroit with predictions. The one in the last paragraph has turned out to be quite accurate.

Wood product mills were closing. One company surveyed the region and found that 25 mills had closed in western Oregon and Washington.[41] The reasons for the closings were not given but the implication was clear— timber supply from federal land was one important causal factor.

Tensions were rising in the late winter and early spring of 1988. The planning process for the national forests was generating all kinds of responses. An all-day emergency conference was held in Portland on March 2.[42] The 'Let's Get a Rope' headline for the story of the meeting in Counterpoint captured the feeling of more than 200 people in attendance at the meeting. Those attending represented the forest products industry and leaders from Oregon's non-timber businesses, and representatives of the Oregon and Washington Congressional delegations. The feeling was that federal forestland was being set aside for everything except jobs. There was a strong sentiment that with the federal government controlling a majority of the standing saw timber in the U. S. the future of the region was largely influenced by federal forest planning. A planned reduction in the availability of federal timber seriously concerned the participants in the conference.

Meanwhile, others were expressing concern that too much old growth would be cut. In a letter addressed to "Dear Oregon Conservationist" James Monteith of the Oregon Natural Resources Center said, "As I write you, the fate of Oregon's old growth forests is the focus of one of this state's most passionate natural resource debates. The rate at which we are losing this priceless resource has accelerated drastically, and if we don't act immediately, this magnificent heritage will be forever lost. The Oregon Natural Resources Council (ONRC) was at the forefront of an unprecedented campaign to protect Oregon's primeval forests."[43] The letter of four pages went on to use statistics that had been challenged time and again to support the contention of ONRC that little old growth remained and had to be protected. The message in Monteith's letter was to join ONRC.

While planning was under way to devise a way to protect the owl and old growth, other information surfaced that was of the good news/bad news sort. On the Rogue River National Forest, in southern Oregon, a Forest Service biologist took a group into the Forest to see a NSO. The forest occupied by the owl was not old growth. A U. S. Fish and Wildlife Service biologist, who was the spotted owl coordinator, told the group that about 10 percent of the population was in non old growth forests.[44]

The State of Oregon formed a task force to review and comment on the plans being developed by the Forest Service. A leader of that task force, Ann Hanus, an economist with the State, reported to a grass roots organization, The Third Force For Forestry, that, "The National Forest Service has a history of tailoring needs to the community. I think the state will have a lot of influence on the proposed forest management plans."[45] As we have seen, other economists were somewhat less sanguine.

Environmentalists were moving on several fronts to protect the NSO. A local Audubon chapter president was interviewed on his perspective on the owl. He was quoted as saying, "If we figure that humans will be here for another 1,000 years, 10 years without logging the land is not that long...I'm more of a conservative environmentalist than most people. Actually I'm probably more of a hard core birder than I am an environmentalist. But the good Lord put us and the owls here together and I don't see it's our place to eliminate another species just because there's money to be made on the trees."[46] To pursue their objective of protecting the owl, Audubon filed a lawsuit in U. S. District Court asking the court to order the U. S. Fish and Wildlife Service to list the owl under the

Endangered Species Act.[47] At the time the Fish and Wildlife Service's position was that it was not necessary to list the species.

The lawsuit was dismissed by U. S. District Judge Helen Frye in Portland. That decision was appealed to the 9th Circuit Court in San Francisco. In the meantime, Senator Mark Hatfield had moved through Congress a bill that blocked the lawsuit; it was that legislation that caused Judge Frye to dismiss the lawsuit. The appeals court ordered the BLM to refrain from letting new contracts to cut old-growth timber on its western Oregon districts pending further hearings. Andy Kerr, ONRC, was sure the appeal would prevail despite Hatfield's efforts. "When it comes to old-growth forests, Hatfield is bad news," Kerr was reported to have said.[48]

The temporary ban on BLM harvests immediately raised concern in the counties where the ban was in effect. The counties in which BLM manages land receive 50% of the timber sale proceeds from BLM in support of county government and schools. Halting timber sales would have a major impact on revenues.[49]

BLM biologists had studied the owl and prepared a report that was completed in May 1987. It was not released to the public. In March 1988 a copy of the report was sent to Vic Sher, an attorney with the Sierra Club Legal Defense Fund in Seattle, according to an article in the Eugene *Register Guard*.[50] The suitable habitat for the owl will decline at a faster rate than acreage of old growth, according to the report, the article says, because fragmenting the forest disrupts the owls' ability to nest and forage. Spotted owl pairs need an average of 2,200 acres of old growth forest in Oregon, according to the report.

The 2,200-acre figure, always given as an average, was rarely if ever accompanied by a statement of the variation around the average. If the variation were quite small, say, 100 acres that would mean one thing. If the variation were quite large, say, 1,000 or 1,500 acres that would mean something quite different. If the variation were 100, then between 2100 and 2300 acres would be needed for each owl pair. If the variation were 1500, then somewhere between 700 and 3700 acres would be needed for each pair. The difference in needed set-aside acreage would be quite large.

The planning process on the national forests, whatever it produced, was likely to have significant impact on the people whose livelihoods depended on timber jobs. James Petersen, editor of *Evergreen*, reported on an incident at a public forum to discuss the proposed plan for the Umpqua National Forest in southern Oregon.[51]

"When Dr. Norm Johnson, the Governor's forest planning guru, was in Roseburg in March, conducting a public hearing concerning the Umpqua National Forest Plan, he was confronted by a young timber faller I doubt he will ever forget.

"The young faller had been unable to testify because preservationists had monopolized the podium, so when Johnson recessed the hearing at about 9:30, the young man approached him and said, 'Dr. Johnson, I have to get up at two in the morning to go to work, so I don't think I can stay any longer; but I just wanted you to know that if the timber harvest level on this forest goes down and I lose my job, my family will starve.'

"I have thought a lot about this young man, who I did not know, since that night in Roseburg. Most of my writing career has been spent chronicling the triumphs and tragedies that frequent ordinary people. I'm not sure why this is, except that I have always had a deep sense of appreciation for life's everyday heroes—those millions of Americans who get up every morning and go to work to earn enough money to feed and clothe their families, pay their bills and, with a little luck, save enough to be able to enjoy their retirement years.

"I suppose the main reason my memory of this young timber faller is still so fresh in my mind is that his job will be one of the first to go if the Umpqua harvest level drops. And if the preservationists have their way, he will be among 2,900 Douglas County workers walking the streets looking for jobs. There won't be any.

"Frankly, I think the preservationists ought to be held accountable for the safety and well being of the families that are made to suffer as a result of their actions. Unfortunately, the law does not provide for this. Indeed, it does not appear that society has any means at hand to hold the preservationists accountable for any of their actions—not the job losses they cause, or their misrepresentation of facts, or their deliberate misuse of a legal system that continues to bend over backward to ensure preservation of preservationists rights.

"What about the rights of decent, hard-working people? Where is their platform? What court hears their grievances? What laws shield them from loss of employment, loss of home or loss of hope?

"Personally, I think this situation has reached the crisis stage here in Oregon. The success of any one of a handful of preservationist strategies—the spotted owl lawsuit filed against the Bureau of Land Management, the buyback timber sale appeals filed against the Forest Service, or the ever-present national park threat—will bring this state's economy crashing down around our ears. Anyone who does not understand this probably also does not understand basic economics, or what makes this state's economy tick.

"The forest planning process is far more important than even the numbers suggest. These plans will set the stage for the kind of growth that occurs in Oregon from this day forward. Unfortunately, the preservationists have a much better understanding of this fact than do ordinary Oregonians. They also do a much better job of courting the news media, which is why it is virtually impossible to find an accurate accounting of the forest planning process or the issues it embraces.

"Two things concern me most about the Umpqua Forest Plan. First, there is the very real danger that preservationists will sabotage it with form letters from afar, just like they did on the Siskiyou National Forest. Second, the battleground we really need to conquer lies far beyond Oregon's borders. Out there, in the plains states and in the industrial towns east of the Mississippi are millions of ordinary Americans, just like us who are convinced the timber industry is destroying the last of the nation's forest reserves.

"Preservationist groups are doing a masterful job of capitalizing on this ignorance. We are going to have to do something about this in the near future, or there will not be a timber industry in Oregon, or anywhere else in America for that matter. If the tide of public opinion should ever turn completely against us, we don't stand a chance. Simply put, there is no condemnation of damning and so final as the condemnation of a nation.

"We face a long uphill battle against a relentless foe whose arrogance, lust for power and disregard for human suffering seem to know no bounds. About all we have left in our own bag of tricks are decency, honesty, and truth. Hopefully, it will be enough." [24]

A decade later we will see that one of the over-riding issues is sustainability. In 1988 the issue was Community Stability. Does the federal government have the responsibility for maintaining a supply of timber from its land so that communities dependent on that timber can have some sort of stability? This was an issue because of the large percentage of land owned by the federal government in states such as Oregon. An economist traced the history of development of the issue in a paper published in mid-1988. [52]

Schallau noted that, "Because of abundant timber on private lands, demand for public stumpage was practically nonexistent until after World War II. The Forest Service could not affect the economic development of timber-dependent communities until it became a significant force in the marketplace for timber products; there was no need for Congress to intervene in the name of community stability." A parallel issue was sustained yield, an idea going back to the Organic Act of 1897 that called for a continuous supply of timber. Schallau points out that these are not necessarily compatible issues. Furthermore, in the years before World War II, industry was not anxious for the national forests to provide another source of raw material that would compete with private timber. How times had changed!

Schallau structured his discussion around a series of questions: Which is more important, sustained yield or community stability? How is community stability achieved? Has community stability acquired economic

standing? Is the Forest Service subsidizing the forest products industry?
What will take the place of the forest products industry? Does the forest
products industry matter? In answering the last question he takes the
discussion to an international level. There he cites studies that show that if
the United States is to maintain preeminence it must maintain mastery and
control of manufacturing production.

Schallau uses a quote to frame his conclusion. We must "avoid the
idiocies that result when we make domestic policy as if our internal choices
had no consequences in international markets...[and] we must link
domestic policy to international policy in a more positive way."[53] Schallau
says, "Finally, I believe we must avoid the idiocies that result when we
make community stability policy as if our choices had no consequences in
regional and national markets."

With hindsight at 20/20 we see that in 1988 at least some people were
sensing that what happened on national forests had both national and
international impacts. Would the policy of protecting the owl at all costs
have consequences on forests in countries with less well developed forest
protection laws? Would the protection of the owl lead to unwanted
changes in the timber dependent communities? We hear much of fragile
ecosystems. If man is included as a component in those ecosystems, a
question must be posed about the resiliency of that species in a world
shaped by forest policies.

In mid-1988 there were no sure figures on the impact of owl protection
on timber harvest. At that time harvest levels on national forests were
high. From 1980 to 1989 harvest levels in Oregon from federal land
averaged over 2.2 billion board feet per year.[54] There were reality checks,
nevertheless. BLM reported that harvest from its land could plummet.[55]

Some had concluded that timber harvest should be stopped, period.
BLM had trees in one of its timber sales spiked.[56] Activity of eco-terrorists
was just beginning. Andy Kerr, of Oregon Natural Resources Council,
reasoned that the tree spikers were frustrated with standard negotiations.[57]

The battle over timber harvest was waged in all venues, from spiking in
the woods to the solemnity of the courts. The spiking of trees slowed the
harvest; a court injunction halted harvest. The injunction was appealed; a
higher court overturned a lower court order. By mid-summer of 1988 the
9th Circuit Court in San Francisco modified an earlier order and let BLM
proceed with some sales provided they kept 2.1 miles away from NSO
nests.[58] The congressional budget process controls the amount of timber
harvested on national forests. While the courts and terrorists were
affecting the harvest the U. S. House of Representatives' subcommittee on
Forest Service budget voted to lower the harvest in Washington and
Oregon from 5.2 to 4.95 billion board feet in 1989 on 19 national forests.
Environmentalists expressed concern that this level was not sustainable and

industry spokesmen expressed fear that the industry could not meet the demand for lumber. [59]

Appeals to the courts were more and more being used to halt action—timber harvest—on federal land. Oregon had a white hat senator, Mark Hatfield. As senior senator he had a well-deserved reputation for doing the right thing. With the appeals being used in ways that the senator believed to go against the best interests of all Oregonians he introduced amendments in a Senate appropriations bill that would limit appeals of Forest Service and BLM management activity. The amendments drew a vigorous protest from environmentalists, and all of a sudden the white hat was black.[60]

In the meantime, eco-terrorists were continuing to use all possible techniques to halt the logging of old growth. *Evergreen* published a special issue that featured an interview with a timber faller.[61] The report begins:

"You could get killed doing what Mark Keiser does for a living. He is a timber faller.

"Next to underground mining, there is no more dangerous profession than timber falling.

"This summer, a deadly new danger waits in the woods for Keiser every morning.

"It is the tree spike—a murderous solid steel shaft driven deep into old growth timber by Earth First! members who oppose timber harvesting.

"Tree spikes—up to 12 inches long—are virtually impossible to detect. When they are driven carefully on a diagonal, downward angle, their nail heads sink deeply into the tree bark, leaving no visible trace of what lies just beneath the outer bark layer.

"Though Keiser's saw has never struck a spike, there is no doubt in his mind what would happen if it did.

"'It would cause the saw to kick back violently, probably into my chest or legs,' he says quietly. 'I don't like to think about it, but I guess every timber faller does.'...

"'This is pretty scary business even under good working conditions,' Keiser continued. 'It requires intense concentration and tremendous physical stamina. You can only do this for five or six hours a day. If you push yourself too hard you make stupid mistakes. Mistakes can kill.'...

"In defense of logging, Keiser offers this very much to the point perspective: 'I don't take these damned logs home with me at night. The American public consumes them in the form of lumber and paper products.' [34]

Some time later environmental activist Edward Abbey was quoted as saying that tree spiking was a valid tactic.[62]

The combination of courts, laws, regulations, agencies, and opponents of the timber industry were hard for some to comprehend. There had been glory days for the timber industry in Oregon. One of the pioneers of that industry felt deep concern for America. He said, "We have an entire generation out there now that does not understand how wealth is created in this world. Our young people need to be taught that our basic industries—timber, mining, agriculture, fishing and oil and gas exploration—are the source of all wealth. Every job on earth results from the conversion of raw material to finished products."[63] It is interesting as we begin the next millennium to try to find an exception to this statement. The links are not always obvious. The information industry depends on mined metals and plastics for the tools it uses. Artists need paint and paper. Service industries use materials from the basic industries, and intellectuals need paper, or computers, or instruments of some kind.

The NSO and old growth forests were the pivotal points of contention. Senator Mark Hatfield met with environmentalists and pleaded for balance.[64] Others sought another way to achieve balance. The Western State Legislative Task Force—representatives from western legislatures—meeting in Lewiston, Idaho—passed a resolution seeking a limit on the size of the acreage set aside for a nesting pair of NSO.[65] Rep. VanLeeuwen had written to the regional forester expressing concern about the acreage being set aside for the NSO pairs. The regional forester wrote to the representative and confirmed the agency's plan to set aside 1,500 acres per pair of NSO.[66] The U. S. Secretary of Agriculture's office confirmed the decision a month later.[67]

Oregon's lumber production had been on an upswing since the low in the early part of the decade. In 1982 the production was 4.68 billion board feet (bbf). That climbed to 7.21 bbf by 1985 and to 8.85 bbf by 1987.[68] Those increasing volumes meant additional money for roads and schools. No wonder legislators were concerned about a reduction in production.

The biologists were holding the line on protecting the owl. One of the leaders, Charles Meslow, spoke at a Third Force for Forestry meeting, and said, "The Spotted Owl is the only animal which will die if all the old growth timber is cut down. I don't feel the Spotted Owl can adapt." [69] Dr. Meslow was director of the Oregon Cooperative Wildlife Research Unit at Oregon State University.

The courts were active also. Up until this time the NSO was a concern, but it had not been listed under the ESA. On November 9, 1988, U. S. District Judge Thomas S. Zilly was quoted as saying the U. S. Fish and Wildlife Service's decision not to designate the northern spotted owl as an endangered species was arbitrary and capricious.[70] At about the same time in another court a jury ordered Earth First! to pay to a logging company $30,000. for locking themselves to their logging equipment in July, 1987.[71] The BLM distributed a news release with the heading, "BLM's Western Oregon Timber Sales to Drop in FY89."[72] Newspaper editors were making their readers aware of what was happening. The Lebanon *Express* ran an editorial headed, "Wood industry hurting if trend not reversed."[73] Private citizens were attempting to alert the people to impending changes. Lynn Buchanan, a Linn County resident, wrote to the *Democrat Herald* and pointed out mill closings due to wilderness and owl protection. The letter concluded by saying, "Get involved. Write the Forest Service. It only takes a minute to let them know you care about your future, which depends on their decisions."[74]

The budget for the Forest Service sheds light on the direction the agency would be going in the near future. Speaking to the Chamber of Commerce in Sweet Home, Senator Hatfield expressed serious concern about the proposed reductions in funds for timber harvest in the federal budget. He assured a local legislator that he would get the funding back up.[75] It was reported that the senator went on to tell the group, "I'm not always going to be there and we can't depend on the bail-out role I play year in and year out." " Unable to win all their battles at the legislative levels, preservationists have turned to the courts, especially the federal ninth Circuit Court," Hatfield said. "We now have the courts becoming involved in the management of forests, not on the basis of sound forestry practices but on a political basis."

The senator continued on the same subject a few days later in Eugene. He was quoted as saying that efforts by environmental groups to protect the spotted owl represent an economic attack on all Oregonians.[76] The senator must have been supported in his stand from letters such as the one from David L. Greer to his local paper. Mr. Greer, after noting that a large mill had closed in Sweet Home due to lack of big logs, went on to say, "Without extremist (sic), there would be no middle of the road. But here is a case where environmental extremists, with literally nothing better to do, have succeeded in destroying many people's lives, to save a lesser species that was never in danger to begin with!"[77] Environmentalists were upset with the senator. "We are shocked by his extreme language, and saddened by his lack of understanding of our concerns," it was reported from Eugene.[78]

Meanwhile the Forest Service was moving ahead to beef up its owl protection efforts. The chief of the Forest Service in Washington, DC reported additional areas would be set aside to protect nesting owls. Areas of from 1,000 to 2,000 acres are to be set-aside in addition to the 1.6 million acres already set aside for owl protection.[79] This plan was immediately criticized by environmentalists who felt the Forest Service was not doing enough to protect the owl.[80]

As the 1988 holiday season approached, timber industry news was not good. The Northwest Forestry Association warned of a timber recession and added that if it did occur the industry would not be able to do a turn-around as it had earlier in the 1980s.[81] At the same time there was some good news: a Sweet Home mill was planning to expand.[82] The mill manufactured wooden windows and door stock.

The Oregon Natural Resources Council filed appeals on six timber sales on the Umpqua National Forest.[83] Those appeals were followed by others that challenged the Forest Service spotted owl management plan.[84]

The year 1988 came to a close with worries about mill closings, lawsuits, future federal timber availability, and, among other things, whether Oregon departments were following legislative intent. Rep. VanLeeuwen wrote to Governor Goldschmidt and pleaded for him to look into the matter of the listing of the spotted owl by the Oregon Department of Fish and Wildlife. The representative cited the Oregon Endangered Species Act, upon which she had voted, and expressed the opinion that the Department had not followed legislative intent.[85]

CHAPTER FIVE

THE ISSUES ARE SHARPENED

"Wilderness and spotted owl not more important than people and the communities." [86] The 65th Oregon Legislative Assembly issued Senate Joint Memorial 15, which urged the U. S. Congress to limit the ability to appeal federal timber sales. The year 1989 was underway.

Robert L. Hill, editor of Oregon Business Magazine said,

"The front pages of major Oregon newspapers this past month have been filled with stories about the Legislature and the battles that will be fought there. At the same time, the inside pages of those newspapers' business sections contained small stories with headlines such as '150 To Be Laid Off by Hampton Affiliates Due To Log Shortages,' 'Governor Asks End To Timber Sales Ban Over Spotted Owl,' 'Log Shortage Closes Simpson Albany Mill, 200 To Be Idled.'

"The biggest fight between the Legislature and governor will be over $225 million, or 4.5% of the general fund budget—the amount Governor Neil Goldschmidt wants that exceeds the spending limit. Yet, at the same time, profound changes are beginning to affect this state's most important industry, changes that will affect billions of dollars and thousands of jobs, reach every corner of the state, and last for decades.

"Because of environmental lawsuits, it is becoming ever more difficult to harvest timber on federal lands, the chief source of logs in this state, while an increasing number of the logs harvested on state and private lands are being exported.

"It is estimated that just the current federal court injunction against logging on Bureau of Land Management (BLM) forests near spotted owl habitat will cost 18 western Oregon counties $50 million this year."[87]

Meanwhile the status of the owl was being re-examined. In 1987 the U. S. Fish and Wildlife Service had ruled that the northern spotted owl did not qualify for listing under the Endangered Species Act. The U. S. District Court had subsequently ruled that the Service should re-evaluate its finding.[88]

By 1989 the Willamette National Forest staff was deeply involved in developing the final draft of the Forest's management plan. The first draft had been out for review and public comment; between December 7, 1987 and May 16, 1988, the Willamette National Forest received about 17,400 pieces of mail containing comments on its draft plan.[89] As noted earlier, a majority of the comments took exception to the Preferred Alternative J. "The difficulty for us lies in the fact that for each issue you've challenged in Alternative J, the opposition to our preferred course of management is pretty well balanced on either 'side of the fence.' While many of you think the Alternative goes too far, many of you also think it doesn't go far enough!"[90]

As we have seen, timber harvesting in the national forests of Oregon began in earnest after World War II. The timber stands in the national forests were varied due to history of disturbance, soils, elevation, exposure and accessibility. Quite naturally, the most accessible and most valuable stands were harvested first. The stands meeting these criteria were older, more mature forests. By 1989 it was not easy to say how many acres of this older forest remained. For example, the amount of old growth on the Willamette National Forest was not known. How much depended on the criteria used to classify the forests.

Potential Mature and Old-Growth Matrix[91]

Willamette National Forest

(Draft—Preliminary Information, April 19, 1989)[1]

Stand Types	Mature and Old-Growth		Old-Growth Definitions		
	Old-Growth and Mature (WNF DEIS)	Old Growth and Mature (MOM Inventory)	R-6 Regional Guide DBH > 32" TPA > 5	Franklin, et al. Task Force DBH > 32" TPA > 8	SAF Old Growth DBH>40" TPA>10
Low Elev. Doug-Fir, W. Hem	582,000 ac.	538,700 ac.	459,000 ac.	407,800 ac.	357,000 ac.
High elev. Mt. Hemlock, True Fir, Doug-fir	286,000 ac.	197,900 ac.	84,900 ac.	69,400 ac.	53,700 ac.
TOTALS	868,000 ac.	736,600 ac.	543,900 ac.	477,200 ac.	410,700 c.

The Willamette National Forest has 1,791, 000 acres. In 1989 the most conservative estimate of the amount of land that had probably not been disturbed by Europeans was over 410,000 acres and the most liberal was 868,000 acres, or just under 50%. Obviously there was more old forest left after nearly a half century of logging than some participants in the old growth argument would have had one believe. The various commentators on the old growth scene—and the spotted owl scene—used the definition and acreage that suited them; there was not common agreement about what was being fought over.

---

[1] MOM = Mature and Overmature, S. A. F. = Society of American Foresters, DBH = diameter at breast height, TPA = Trees Per Acre, ac.= acres.

As we will see time and again, individuals frequently caught the essence of the argument. One such case was John Kunzman, Sweet Home, OR, who spoke at a rally in 1989. He had this to say:

"Who am I and why am I here?

"My name is John Kunzman: I am a son of Oregon, and God's child. I was born in the timber town of Molalla and raised on the fruits of love from timber dependent families.

"My life's travels have brought me to another timber town. My work and play; my home and my love now have deep roots in timber dependent Sweet Home!

"With these truths, I make the following remarks today:

"We have no conclusive evidence that spotted owls are declining or increasing...

"We really don't know how many owls there are and we don't know where they are...

We know that there are more owls than we once thought!

"We know that their habitat is much more diverse than we once thought!

"We now know that they live in small fragmented patches of timber and that they frequently fly into second growth timber.

"We know that we have 4.2 million acres of old growth timber in Oregon and Washington federal land set aside as wilderness, National Parks, roadless, scenic and other preserves where timber harvest is not permitted. EVER!!!...we have not looked for spotted owls in these areas.

"We know that we have 3.3 million acres of unreserved old growth timber now standing in Oregon and Washington's federal lands. At our present rate of production, we calculate that it would take 60 years to harvest.

"I simply feel that there's enough room in the woods for Loggers and Owls.

"In conclusion, I say:

"We are Oregon's First Families! Please don't let us become a liability to this country when we have been an asset for so long.

"Please don't define the owl as an enemy. We wish to co-exist with it!

"For our sake and the sake of the owl, put man back into the environmental equation where he belongs." [92]

Mr. Kunzman spoke from the heart and expressed sentiments that were widespread in the communities dependent on federal timber. At the same time environmental groups, some quite radical, were leaving no stone unturned to stop all logging on federal land. The Associated Oregon Loggers put together a collection of papers under the heading, "Prevent Environmental Sabotage Today" (PEST). The collection included several documents from Earth First! describing techniques for sabotaging logging equipment. It also included an interview of Dave Foreman, Founder of Earth First! by Jerry Mason of the Willamette National Forest. The interview captures the feeling that existed then and to a large degree now in some sectors of the environmental movement.[93]

Mason: For background, tell us why you decided Earth First! needed to be formed. What were the reasons for the birth of Earth First!?

Foreman: In a word—RARE II. As one of the four national RARE II coordinators for the Wilderness Society and Sierra Club (the others were Tim Mahoney, Doug Scott, and John McComb), I was devastated by the results announced by the Forest Service in January 1979. I had worked through the system; for over 8 years on Forest Service Wilderness issues—I was at the time the chief lobbyist for the Wilderness Society in Washington, DC. We had played the RARE II game honestly by the Forest Service rules, we had been moderate, reasonable, professional and factual instead of emotional. And we lost. Out of 66 million acres in RARE II and another 14 or 15 million acres of roadless areas already dropped through unit plans, only 15 million were recommended for wilderness by the Forest Service. And that 15 million acres largely consisted of rocks and ice—areas without supposed economic conflicts. The Forest Service demonstrated in RARE II their utter devotion to the conversion of unlogged forest into managed tree farms and to the destruction of de facto wilderness.

Mason: How did Earth First! actually come into existence?

Foreman: Following RARE II, a number of people in national and state conservation groups began to discuss the need for a more hard-line group. At first, it was something of a bitter joke that we needed something to offset extremists in the timber, mining, livestock and other industries. But eventually some of us began to recognize that we—the conservation movement—were to blame. We had compromised, we had sold out, we had accepted anthropocentric "resourcism" as the basis for argument. Finally, in April of 1980, four friends and I went to the Pinacate Desert of Mexico for a backpack trip. We decided on that trip to quit talking and do something. Of the five of us, two worked for The Wilderness Society, one for Friends of the Earth, one was a Forest Service employee, and the other an oil field roughneck.

Mason: How is Earth First! organized? And how is it different than other more traditional organizations?

Foreman: One of the problems we saw was that conservation organizations were organized like corporations. When you're organized like a corporation, we reasoned, you think and act like a corporation. The Sierra Club, we felt, had become more "club" than "sierra", the Wilderness Society, more "society" than "wilderness." Hierarchy had set in, there was a division between professional staff and grassroots. We wanted to avoid the pitfalls of organization and administrative overhead. The only model we had for the kind of organization we wanted was the hunter-gatherer tribe, the social organization that has served human beings for 95 percent of our time. We have leadership, yes, but it is an informal leadership that comes from respect within the group and not because of holding some formal organizational position.

Mason: What were the original purposes for Earth First!? Have they changed much since it was originally conceived?

Foreman: The purposes for Earth First! originally were multifold:

- to reintroduce humor and passion into the boring environmental movement;
- to introduce non-violent civil disobedience into the cause of wilderness preservation;
- to articulate non-anthropocentric arguments for wilderness preservation;
- to redefine wilderness from a standpoint of biological diversity rather than of recreation;
- to restructure the terms of the conservation debate;
- to offer constructive internal criticism of mainstream environmental groups;
- to expand the terms of the wilderness discussion away from mere preservation of what is still wild to a visionary view of wilderness restoration involving a million acres or more and reintroduction of all native wildlife.

Those purposes have not changed since our beginning, although some may have different emphases today.

Mason: What is your role in Earth First!?

Foreman: My role is changing. Since 1980, I have been the primary national spokesperson for Earth First! and probably the most influential person in the movement. I have recently handed over the editorship of "The Earth First! Journal" to John Davis and am trying to move out of my "leadership" role in the movement. I'm doing that for several reasons: first, while it was necessary to get Earth First! off the ground to have a strong "leader", it is not necessary now. It's better for leadership to become much more decentralized in-the-group today. And secondly, all my adult life, I've spoken for a group. I want the freedom now to speak just for myself.

Mason: What, in your opinion, has Earth First! achieved since it was founded?

Foreman: We have established civil disobedience as an effective and legitimate tool for preservation of natural diversity. We have certainly popularized monkeywrenching. We have put some pizzazz back into the conservation movement and have caused the media to begin covering environmental issues to a greater degree. We have also, I think, redefined the terms of the debate and have restructured the environmental spectrum. Nobody, for example, thinks of the Sierra Club as being extreme any longer. People are discussing preservation of all old growth forests now, they are discussing wilderness restoration, and natural diversity is being thought of more as the reason for wilderness preservation than is recreation. Of course, we aren't entirely responsible for all of this, but Earth First! has played a significant role.

Mason: How would you describe the reaction of other groups, the Forest Service included, to Earth First!s existence and actions?

Foreman: Mixed! While some in the Forest Service, and even in conservation groups, condemn us, others are strong supporters. I think you would be surprised to know how many people in the Forest Service are highly sympathetic to Earth First!.   We initially became involved in the Bald Mountain Road controversy because several professional staff people on the Siskiyou National Forest <u>invited us</u> to do <u>so.</u> We receive a lot of information and money from Forest Service employees who are disgusted with the current direction of the agency.

Mason: What actions have worked best to meet your purposes?

Foreman: I believe in using the whole toolbox. We need scientists in and out of the Forest Service researching the values and complexity of old growth forests, for example. We need the Nature Conservancy buying key tracts for preservation. We need the Sierra Club and Wilderness Society lobbying. Preparing research papers. Filing appeals and lawsuits. In Earth First! we write letters, file appeals and lawsuits, develop visionary wilderness proposals, comment on EISs, even lobby.   Earth First!ers also demonstrate, sit in front of bulldozers, climb trees; and of course there are folks who, as a last resort, go out and pull up survey stakes, decommission bulldozers, and the like.

Mason: How does Earth First! work in conjunction with other environmental groups?

Foreman: Earth First! has its special role within the conservation movement.   We do not join coalitions because we aren't willing to compromise. We do, however, discuss issues with individuals in other groups and try to complement their strategy whenever possible.

Mason: What are the three main goals of Earth First as it looks into the 1990s?

Foreman: It would be hard to speak for the Earth First! movement on that score, but my three main goals would be to reduce human population to about 100 million worldwide, destroy the industrial infrastructure, and see wilderness with its full complement of species returning throughout the world. Obviously, that's not going to happen because of anything I do, but it may be the result of what industrial society does to itself.

Mason: Please describe a likely environmental and political scenario with respect to 1) the forest environment in the Pacific Northwest and 2) the world ecosystem if current trends continue as they have in the 80's through the 1990s.

Foreman: #1 - Appalachia

#2 - Ethiopia, Bangladesh, Mexico City

Mason: The subjects of monkeywrenching and ecotage are terms associated with Earth First! Would you describe what these terms mean to you and why they are employed? Also are there some key misconceptions others may have about such practices?

Foreman: You need to read the section on monkeywrenching in "Ecodefense: a Field Guide to monkeywrenching" [SEE ELEMENTS OF MONKEYWRENCHING ATTACHED]

The key misconceptions about monkeywrenching are that it is violent or that it is mindless vandalism. It is non-violent in that it is directed only towards inanimate objects and not towards people; and it's very deliberate and done as a last resort. Calling monkeywrenching "terrorism" makes the word "terrorism" meaningless. The contras are "freedom fighters" and someone who pulls up a survey stake is a "terrorist"? That's absurd! Of course, King George III would have called people involved with the Boston Tea Party, and later George Washington himself, "terrorists" if he had such a handy label.

Mason: What does Earth First! gain by ecotage and monkeywrenching? What does it lose?

Foreman: Earth First! as a group does not engage in monkeywrenching for obvious reasons. Individuals who are involved in Earth First! may monkeywrench, however. That may seem like a rhetorical difference only, but it is an important one. The main thing a monkeywrencher gains is wilderness—some areas will be preserved because of the practice. What Earth First! would lose by monkeywrenching would be a loss of credibility within the political process by not playing the game according to the rules set up for us. However. I don't consider that would be much of a loss.

Mason: Please clarify the difference between free speech, civil disobedience, and monkeywrenching in philosophy and practice.

Foreman: I don't really see where free speech fits into this question, but the difference between civil disobedience and monkeywrenching in my mind, is that a philosophical adherent to classical civil disobedience (Gandhian non-violence) is primarily interested in her or his moral statement and not in the results. A monkeywrencher is interested in the results and not in chalking up brownie points in heaven. In practice, someone involved in civil disobedience wants to be arrested. Obviously a monkeywrencher does not want to be arrested.   Moreover, a civil disobedience person is trying to reform the existing system by her or his actions; a monkeywrencher is trying to thwart the system. Those who feel more strongly about civil disobedience would no doubt disagree with me on these points and I recognize that some people involved in civil disobedience do it from the strategic perspective of monkey wrenching. While I once was a strong proponent of civil disobedience, I am much less enthusiastic about it today. Non-violent, non-revolutionary, "friendly" monkeywrenching is what I think is most effective.

Mason: Do you think people in the Forest Service correctly interpret Earth First!'s interests, comments, and actions? If not, what can be done to correct the misconceptions?

Foreman: Certainly some people in the Forest Service correctly interpret Earth First!s interests, actions, and comments. They largely support us. I don't think it is possible for many in the Forest Service to understand Earth First! because we are approaching "management" of the National Forests from an entirely different worldview than they are. The orientation of the Forest Service is humanism—standard of value is the human being, all problems are solvable by human beings, resources or their substitutes are infinite. Our orientation is biocentrism—meaning all forms of life have intrinsic value, communities are more important than individuals, all things are interconnected, and human beings have overshot their carrying capacity.

Mason: What are the main motivations of people who align themselves with Earth First!?

Foreman: An absolute love and passion for the natural world. Wilderness, the flow of evolution.

Mason: What are some of the main frustrations Earth First! folks have with the U.S. Forest Service?

Foreman: Apart from the obvious ones of differing world views and the Forest Service's commitment to large timber corporations and wealthy ranchers, our frustration is with those employees of the Forest Service who know that the current direction of the Forest Service is wrong and who don't have the personal courage or integrity to do something about it.

Mason: Given the decision framework within which we operate, what reasonable changes would you advocate that the Forest Service make to be more responsive to Earth First! concerns?

Foreman: I generally agree with Howie Wolke's proposals included in an Earth First! tabloid about the Forest Service [see VISION: A BIOCENTRIC PROPOSAL FOR THE NATIONAL FORESTS— ATTACHED] although they are relatively moderate from our perspective. One could argue that even more roads need to be closed, and that there should be no timber cutting at all on National Forests.

Mason: The Forest Service strives to be responsive to all its stockholders, but cannot fully satisfy all the increasing demands. What would you do if you were Chief of the Forest Service to respond to these demands?

Foreman: The Chief should take immediate and personal responsibility for the fact that the United States Forest Service is one of the leading entities in the world today responsible for the greatest extinction crisis in the history of this planet and for the worldwide devastation of native diversity and its conversion to artificial "neo-Europes". He should take whatever measures are necessary to turn the agency and its destructive management around, and to protect the National Forests as crucial reserves of native diversity.

Mason: Describe the successes of Earth First! so far and future successes you are hoping for.

Foreman: We have had virtually no successes, in my opinion, and we are unlikely to have any successes. The next half-century is going to make the fall of Rome look like a picnic. We may lose over one-third of all species on the planet. The Greenhouse Effect and depletion of the ozone layer, along with major climatic disruption and die-off of species, is going to devastate the Earth we know. We are in the middle of the greatest crisis of three and a half billion years of life on Earth and nearly everybody is pretending it's not happening. The U.S. Forest Service is directly responsible for the damage done to the forest, woodland, and grassland ecosystems of the National Forests, and for the destruction of the most diverse, complex, and beautiful coniferous forest on Earth—that of the Pacific Coast.

Mason: This is your opportunity to communicate directly to real people behind the USFS badges. What specific closing message do you want them to hear from the founder of Earth First!?

Foreman: What is your legacy going to be? A wilderness of stumps and raw, bleeding hillsides? or complex, functioning forest ecosystems? Thousands of miles of dusty roads leading nowhere? or productive, healthy Grizzly and Elk habitat?

Are you going to take an ethical stand for life, for the wholeness and integrity of natural ecosystems? or are you going to succumb to the banality of evil and continue to oversee the destruction of native diversity on the National Forests?

END OF INTERVIEW -

Reaction or comments can be sent to Jerry Mason. Public Affairs Officer. Willamette National Forest, P. O. Box 10607. Eugene, OR 97440 or to Dave Foreman, Earth First!, P. O. Box 5871, Tucson, AZ 85703.

The Forest Service was trying to understand what sort of mind-set the people with Earth First! had. The interview was a major step in that direction. The document with the interview also contained a three-page definition of monkeywrenching. The material came from an Earth First! document entitled "Ecodefense" and contained this definition:

"It is time for women and men, individually and in small groups, to act heroically and admittedly illegally in defense of the wild, to put a monkeywrench into the gears of the machine destroying natural diversity. Strategic monkeywrenching can be safe, easy and fun, but most importantly it can be effective in stopping timber cutting, road building, overgrazing, oil & gas exploration, mining, dam building, overgrazing (sic), power line construction, off-road vehicle use, trapping, ski area development, and other forms of destruction of the wilderness. But it must be strategic, it must be thoughtful, it must be deliberate in order to succeed. Such a campaign of resistance would follow these principles:
Monkeywrenching is Non-Violent
Monkeywrenching is Not Organized
Monkeywrenching is Individual
Monkeywrenching is Targeted
Monkeywrenching is Timely
Monkeywrenching is Dispersed
Monkeywrenching is Diverse
Monkeywrenching is Fun
Monkeywrenching is Not Revolutionary
Monkeywrenching is Simple
Monkeywrenching is Deliberate and Ethical"

Each of the principles was followed by a full paragraph explaining the rationale. The whole was summarized thus:

"A movement based on these principles could protect millions of acres of wilderness more stringently than any Congressional act, could insure the propogation (sic) of the grizzly and other threatened life forms better than an army of game wardens, and could lead to the retreat of industrial civilization from large areas of forest, mountain, desert, plain, seashore, swamp, tundra, and woodland that are better suited to the maintenance of natural diversity than to the production of raw materials for over consumptive technological human society.

"If loggers know that a timber sale is spiked, they won't bid on the timber. If a Forest Supervisor knows that road will be continually destroyed, he won't try to build it. If seismographers know that they will be constantly harrassed (sic) in an area, they'll go elsewhere. If ORVers know that they'll get flat tires miles from nowhere, they won't drive in such areas.

"John Muir said that if it ever came to a war between the races, he would side with the bears. That day has arrived."

Certainly this view of the world is diametrically opposed to that expressed by Hill and Kunzman. And just as certainly, it was a view of the

45

world that drew to it large numbers of people with lots of money and diverse feelings about what America was like in the late 20th century.

The concerns raised by these divergent points of view were evident in many ways. A timber worker in a timber dependent community expressed himself this way:

"Editor:

"I write as an employee of North Santiam Plywood where I have worked for more than 24 years. I have lived in the Mill City area for the past 30 years. My kids and my grandkids have been and are being raised here.

"My family and thousands of other families in the length and breadth of this, the North Santiam Canyon, are and hopefully can continue to keep the timber industry alive for many years to come.

"And now we have a group of people who want to put all of us out of work because of a little bird called the Spotted Owl. These people call themselves preservationists. If they get their way, then we the people of the logging and timber industry will be the ones that are threatened and endangered, because if there is no work there is no income and places to live. Mill City, Gates, Detroit and other towns in the canyon become ghost towns. Or is that what they want?

"A vast majority of these people work for the state or federal government with large incomes and with little or no concern for the mill worker and loggers that will lose their jobs. The forest service, both state and federal, have a replanting program that has and will continue to produce more and better timbers for generations to come. And with controlled harvests, several million of us timber workers can't be wrong!"[94]

At about the same time a unit of the University of Oregon published a paper dealing with the same basic subject: How shall the policy of forest use be addressed? The author, Con H. Schallau, was then with the Pacific Northwest Forest Experiment Station. Dr. Schallau is an economist. He looked at the problem from a macroeconomic perspective. In the Executive Summary he had this to say:

"Oregon is at an important crossroad regarding the management of its public forest resources. The issue is whether these resources can support current use: competing interests are seeking the same land—all forest resources are scarce. A decision to allocate more resources to amenity use, for example, means less for alternative uses unless technological developments can increase the productivity of existing resources.

"In the near future, the major decisions regarding Oregon's use of forest resources will relate to the use of public lands managed by the U.S. Forest Service (hereafter referred to as the Forest Service) and the U.S. Bureau of Land Management (BLM). A proactive stance by Oregonians is the only way to assure that the fate of Oregon's economy—particularly in nonmetropolitan areas—and issues regarding environmental consequences of current use of forest land are addressed appropriately.

"The issues are complex and the stakes are high. The economic future of many timber-dependent communities will be in limbo until issues regarding the use of federal forest resources have been resolved. Fortunately, however, Oregon is not faced with an imminent timber famine or an environmental crisis. For this reason, resource managers should avoid a simple solution—Oregonians need not panic. Provided management and scientific skills are allocated appropriately, environmental degradation and economic trauma can be avoided.

"Most Oregonians are aware of the major problems facing forest resources managers. Consequently, more emphasis should be devoted to finding solutions. Unfortunately, time and resources that otherwise could be directed to sustaining the productivity of all forest resources are being dissipated by legal disagreements over current use of Oregon's forest lands. Experiences in the Puget Sound area of Washington suggest that it would better serve citizens of Oregon if mediation, rather than litigation, were used to resolve differences between timber, fishery, and environmental interests."[95]

By early 1989 the Forest Service and BLM were actively fine-tuning their management plans, workers were scared stiff, environmentalists had an issue that could be used to close logging on the federal land, and politicians and policy analysts were seeking common ground. As the 1980s were coming to a close it was not clear what the outcome of the battle over federal land management would be.

CHAPTER SIX

EARLY 1989

1989 dawned bright and not so clear. Opinions varied widely on the status and condition of the timber industry. After some years of recovery following the recession earlier in the decade, the industry had expanded toward the end of the decade and harvest from federal land peaked in 1988. The view of the future depended on your point of view. Environmental groups were using more and more court appeals to halt harvesting on federal land. Senator Bob Packwood called for a ban on forest appeals.[96] An industry group in Washington, DC predicted there would be more layoffs in the timber industry.[97] It was reported that Governor Neil Goldschmidt supported lifting the ban on federal timber sales.[98] Michael Donnelly wrote to the editor of the Salem *Statesman-Journal* pointing out that an earlier letter with some numbers was erroneous—that the timber industry and its employees were greatly overstated.[99] A week later Bruce Harris wrote to the same paper. He had this to say:

"Mr. Donnelly can quote all the statistics he wants to. But this isn't about numbers. It's about people's lives.

"People like Donnelly love to talk about jobs lost or timber barons and large corporations because it hides the ugly truth behind their belief, a belief that says a tree or an owl is worth more to them than the thousands of men, women and children whose survival depends on a healthy timber industry.

"We are the people the environmentalists don't want you to see. We are the ones who will pay the price for their actions.

"They would have you believe that their battle is with the millionaires and wealthy corporations, but they won't be the ones who get hurt. They won't be the ones standing in the unemployment line, losing their homes or trying to support a family on those minimum-wage tourist jobs Donnelly seems so proud of.

"We who live and work in the Santiam Canyon care deeply about the future of the forests and wildlife. After all, it's our home.

"There is room for both recreation and a managed timber harvest, but not for the radicals on either side."[100]

Letters touch on the human and owl side of the issue. For the people on the ground the biology of the owl is in dispute. From Sweet Home, a truly dependent timber town, Jerry Underwood had this to say:

"Enough is enough.

"This letter is directed to the head of the Forest Service and to all of the environmentalists who forced the setting-aside of thousands of acres of old-growth timber lands to ensure that the spotted owls would not become extinct.

"They have said the owl can't exist in low-land, second-growth timber in spite of numerous sightings of spotted owls actually nesting and rearing their young right here on the valley floor. They claim they must have old-growth timber in high elevations to survive. If this is a fact, then why aren't they up there now in the 140 inches of snow, instead of being sighted all winter long in low-land, second-growth stands?

"With six mills already down, three on a curtailed status and the recent announcement of Simpson closing in Albany, for a total of over 1200 jobs, enough is enough.

"We need our timber for our livelihoods and to be able to provide educations for our children. Let's let Mother Nature take care of the spotted owls and turn our attention to the exportation of logs. If this continues, it will eventually turn Oregon into a ghost state."[101]

Others were less pessimistic about the future of forestry in Oregon. Barte Starker, Executive Vice President, Starker Forests, and a member of the State Board of Forestry, spoke to a meeting of the Third Force For Forestry in Lebanon. He told the group that he was optimistic regarding the forest products industry in Oregon.[102]

Editorial writers seem to enjoy getting into a fray such as the owl vs. timber debate. The Albany *Democrat Herald* editorialized about the conflict in this way:

"Mill closures hurt the case for logging

"By closing mills and throwing people out of work right and left, the wood-products industry is weakening its case for continued harvests of public timber.

"From Sweet Home and Lebanon to Harrisburg and Albany, as well as elsewhere in the valley, timber companies have closed mills lately or announced impending closures. Several hundred jobs are going up in smoke.

"One of the reasons usually cited by the owners for curtailing operations has been that federal timber was becoming harder to get. They have blamed appeals of timber sales by radical environmentalists, as well as the pending forest plans, which likely will reduce the annual cuts in the Willamette National Forest and the other federal forests.

"Sometimes the companies' attacks on conservationists, as symbolized by the spotted owl and efforts to save old-growth forests, tend to overshadow other causes of the cutbacks. There is, for instance, a long-term trend toward more automation in Oregon's wood mills. This results in more efficient mills but fewer individual plants and fewer jobs.

"The fewer jobs are left in western Oregon mills, the weaker is the argument that federal timber harvest should be maintained at all costs, or even increased. If the trend is toward ever fewer mills and jobs, then what's the point in logging many of the remaining old trees? By the time second growth comes along, the mills will be gone.

"There are good arguments for keeping the wood industry going at least at the present level, and the Forest Service should not hasten the industry's demise by putting unreasonable restrictions on its sales program. After all, this is supposed to be the best tree-growing region in the world, whole communities in this area still live off the forest, and a whole lot of human beings in these towns are dependent on the forests and the mills.

"Knowing this, the industry should be slower than it is in shutting down mills and abolishing jobs. The more mills close, the fewer people will be left to argue for a sensible policy in the woods."[103]

Being internally consistent is not a prerequisite to editorializing. Automation resulted in fewer mills and the craftsmen needed to supply the mills. The amount of wood needed was the same, however, not less.

Representative VanLeeuwen was responding to the flood of information she was receiving. On its editorial page the Sweet Home *New Era* reported on her activity regarding the owl and national forest management:

Timber Talk

Rep. VanLeeuwen calls for action on owl fiasco

Rep. Liz VanLeeuwen, R., Halsey, is calling upon Governor Goldschmidt to take a leadership role to protect the "Oregon Comeback."

"In Portland layoffs and shutdowns may only cause small tremors. In our rural areas, layoffs and shutdowns are major earthquakes for the total economy," explains VanLeeuwen.

"There is room in the woods for all of us," Rep. VanLeeuwen said Wednesday in Salem.

"I've had calls from discouraged processors and loggers, uncertain about when or if logs will be available for our mills, and now a major retailer has called to say they are unable to place short-term orders for finished wood products because of uncertainty in the log supply," VanLeeuwen said.

Citing a recent Oregon Fish and Wildlife Commission listing of the Northern Spotted Owl as a Threatened Species as a further reason for the uncertainty in the timber industry, VanLeeuwen is calling for immediate and decisive action from the Governor's office to prevent severe economic dislocations in Oregon. "Unless this unnecessary erosion of the available timber supply is reversed, there will be no 'Oregon Comeback', " she asserts.

"In Linn County, there has been a 28% reduction in the available supply of raw materials just from Bureau of Land Management (BLM) lands alone," VanLeeuwen said. "It's getting so bad that we are losing even our local markets to the Canadians and other foreign producers because Oregon manufacturers cannot guarantee retailers they can process their orders."

"We don't have to choose between owls and people in Oregon," said VanLeeuwen. According to United States Forest Service (USFS) and BLM* figures, there are already over 213,000 acres within Linn County which cannot be harvested at this time. That's about 2 1/3 acres for every Linn County resident. "I am working with a number of my colleagues on this artificial timber shortage. Most rural representatives are keenly aware of the devastating impact this is beginning to have in their areas," she said.

The timber recession of the early 80's, was caused by poor market conditions. Unless the current timber supply situation is reversed, we will be creating a recession of as great or greater proportions than that of less than a decade ago.

The supply is here. Oregon has more softwood trees of harvestable size than all 12 southern states combined. This is a political, not a physical shortage of trees. Those who are most vocal in our society have just succeeded in getting government to be more interested in saving a large number of spotted owls than in saving our timber towns and their people. "We just cannot afford to ignore the human consequence any longer," says VanLeeuwen.

VanLeeuwen is asking the Governor to put the following three-point plan into immediate action:

1. Complete the state review of the Federal Forest Service planning documents, carefully considering the long-range harvest history, not that of the timber depression years.

2. Work with the Oregon Fish & Wildlife Commission to reconsider their recent decision in listing the spotted owl as a Threatened Species. VanLeeuwen says she believes the Agency violated the 1987 Endangered Species Act in the procedure or lack of procedure, they used in making their November 18th decision.

3. Encourage Oregon's Congressional delegation to minimize frivolous appeals and lawsuits affecting federal timber sales.

"Trees are a renewable natural resource. With proper management we can keep a continuous supply available for harvest, provide habitat for wildlife and recreational opportunities for our people.

"If the Governor is serious about completing 'Oregon Comeback,' he must take action now, to ensure that we don't fall back into another timber-driven recession that will erase the economic gains Oregonians have worked so hard to accomplish," VanLeeuwen emphasized.

"There are 5,800 acres of BLM land permanently set aside as habitat for 12 pair of spotted owl and an additional 8,200 acres of older growth timber cannot be harvested due to a court injunction because of 38 more pair of spotted owls."[104]

There was no shortage of opinions on how the federal land should be managed. Presumably the National Forest Management Act sets in motion the process for determining public opinion. Public opinion should be a strong element in the process to decide how to manage public land. National forests are frequently referred to as being owned by all citizens—the stakeholders. Late in the 1980s the strength of public opinion was more and more evident. The trouble was that public opinion was not unanimous—differences were to be found. An editorial in *Evergreen* spelled out the sources of difference:

The February 6 issue of *Newsweek* magazine features the most livable cities in America.

"Not surprisingly, our own Portland, Oregon is among the chosen few, judged by *Newsweek* writer Tony Clifton to be one of the finest cities in the nation.

"Clifton's Portland profile begins with a powerful statement I want to share with you.

"In the heart of Portland, Oregon's elegantly restored city center sits Skidmore Fountain, a bronze art nouveau treasure. The inscription chiseled into the six-sided stone base epitomizes the Portland ethos: 'Good citizens are the riches of a city.'"

"The bronze inscription might well have been paraphrased to read, "Good citizens are the riches of a state," for it is a matter of history that Portland's elegance has blossomed from the sweat of loggers, millworkers and farmers who reside in rural Oregon where there are no bronze fountains and where good citizens are not enjoying the riches of the state.

"I am deeply troubled by the division that separates urban Portland from rural Oregon where our state's economic engines, timber and agriculture, reside. A small portion of this division exists naturally, the result of differences in chosen lifestyles, rural and urban. But the chasm that now divides us threatens to undermine the basic building blocks of our state's economy, building blocks that are most visible in Portland where our state's banking, finance, transportation and utility industries are headquartered, and where charitable support for the arts and the humanities is most in evidence.

"Every economic analysis ever done in Oregon confirms that Portland, our state's center of commerce, derives most of its economic vitality from the vitality of our two basic industries, timber and agriculture. Economists are, for example, in agreement that the recovery of Oregon's forest products industry led Oregon out of the recession.

"Unfortunately, this truth rarely surfaces in news accounts that focus on the urban debate over use and management of publicly owned forest and farmlands in rural Oregon. The very visible results of Portland's economic boom have overshadowed the power *behind* the city's rebirth, specifically the conversion of Oregon's farm and forest products into finished goods which are in increasingly high demand in the United States and around the world.

"What is most troubling about this lack of basic economic understanding is the urban-inspired quest to control rural Oregon, as though rural Oregon were Portland's playground; when, in fact, rural Oregon is Portland's workshop. It is where goods are fashioned from natural resources, where the good citizens of rural Oregon fashion our state's riches from the sweat of their brow.

"The recent formation of the Ancient Forest Alliance, which is headquartered in Portland, is an excellent example of this most troubling situation. The Alliance, a powerful new coalition led by the National Audubon Society, the Sierra Club, the Wilderness Society, and the National Wildlife Federation, has a single purpose: to build overwhelming urban support for its proposed ban on the harvest of old-growth timber from publicly-owned forest lands in Oregon and Washington.

"Before it can achieve this end, the Alliance must first convince urban Oregon and Washington that the rural-based forest products industry is in decline and that it is no longer important to the economic future of the Pacific Northwest. I just wish some of our region's more thoughtful journalists would dig into this situation, because you don't have to dig very deeply to discover that our region's future can be made much brighter by nurturing our forest products industry, rather than by trying to destroy it by limiting its access to the God-given productivity of our forests.

"In his recent speech before the Association of Oregon Counties, Oregon's senior Senator Mark Hatfield termed the Alliance strategy, 'an attack on all Oregonians.'

" 'There are many who do not share the values we hold important,' Hatfield said. 'These people have little or no stake in the outcome of the conflict they cause. In fact, many times I'm not sure these people have any understanding or appreciation of the effect these actions have on Oregon and Oregonians-our human resources, our most important resource.'

"Rural Oregonians—good citizens, one and all—know exactly what Senator Hatfield meant, for they are increasingly the victims of urban-inspired political processes that are squandering the economic and spiritual riches of our state." [105]

Signed: Jim Petersen

Mr. Petersen describes his organization thus: "The Evergreen Foundation is a national, non-profit forestry research and education organization, dedicated to the advancement of science based forestry. The Foundation publishes *Evergreen*, a bimonthly journal designed to keep our members, and others, abreast of issues and events impacting forestry, forest communities and the forest products industry.

"*Evergreen* was founded in 1985. Startup funding came from a group of Southern Oregon lumber companies interested in promoting citizen participation in the federal government's forest planning and public involvement processes. In subsequent years, the magazine has assumed a much wider role, providing credible national and international forums for scientists, policy makers and community leaders who share the Foundation's commitment to science-based forestry. As a result, what was once a small regional forestry magazine is today the most widely read forestry journal in the world, with readership in 50 states and 26 countries." [106]

The Evergreen Foundation lived up to its mission by publishing an essay by the Executive Director of the Douglas Timber Operators, a southern Oregon industry association. In the essay, that looks at all sides of the NSO issue, Troy Reinhart had this to say:

"One of the underlying problems with the growing debate over the harvest of old-growth timber from public forest lands in Oregon and Washington is that there is no single, scientifically accepted definition of the term 'old growth.'

"Indeed, it seems that the true meaning or significance of old growth lies more in the mind of the beholder than it does in the minds of scientists who are now being asked to craft a definition that somehow bridges the science and the symbolism of ancient forests.

" Three broad-based descriptions of old growth are at the forefront of the ancient forest debate. These descriptions are the work of the Forest Service, the Society of American Foresters, and, most recently, the Wilderness Society.

"The Forest Service has crafted its definition of old growth around four criteria it believes best describe the ecological conditions present in old-growth forests. These conditions or characteristics include the size of the area which contains mature and over-mature trees, the number of trees in various age classes which are found in the area, the presence and volume of dead standing and on-the-ground timber, and the absence or minimal presence of human activity that would otherwise significantly alter the overall character of the old-growth stand.

"Based on its four-part definition, the Forest Service estimates that the 19 national forests of Oregon and Washington, which cover 24.3 million acres, include 6.2 million acres of old growth. The Wilderness Society disagrees, and on the basis of its own definition, accuses the Forest Service of over-inflating the amount of old growth remaining in the region's national forests by a factor of more than 100%. To this, it should be added that the Wilderness Society's more limiting definition of old growth fits neatly within the organization's strategy for banning the harvest of all remaining publicly-owned old-growth timber.

"Given the very self-serving nature of the Society's definition, it seems more prudent to accept the Forest Service's current definition of old growth. Of the 6.2 million acres of old growth the Forest Service counts, 3.2 million acres are already set-aside in preserves where no timber harvesting will ever be permitted. The remaining 3 million acres, which are the focal point of the current debate, are still available for harvest, and are currently being harvested at a rate of about 1.5 % per year. When this harvest is complete, in about 50 years, the Pacific Northwest will still have its 3.2 million acres of old growth, preserved in perpetuity in parks, wilderness areas and other administrative set-asides designed to protect scenic vistas, wildlife habitat and water quality.

"The 3 million acres of old growth scheduled for harvest over the next 50- plus years will give way to a new forest, planted under the strict control of regulatory processes like the Oregon Forest Practices Act, which ensure that harvested forest lands are successfully planted within three years.

"The bottom line issue in the debate over the continued harvest of old growth is, in my view, control of the 3-million-acre land base on which *unreserved* old-growth timber is standing. Simply put, he who controls this land base and the manner in which it is managed controls our region's forest future.

"In its quest to block the harvest of old-growth Douglas fir from the forests of Oregon and Washington, the National Audubon Society has worked hard to harness the power of the society's reverence for ancient forests. To do this, they have painted an ecologically incorrect, but emotionally powerful, picture of a forest that never really existed here in the west, save for the Sequoias of northern California. The oldest among the Sequoias were young when the Holy Roman Empire embraced all of the known world 2000 years ago. Many more were young when the fiery eruption of Mount Vesuvius destroyed the Roman city of Pompeii in 79 AD

"Douglas fir differ from Sequoias and their Redwood cousins in two important ways. First, lifespan. While there are a few 4,000-year-old Sequoias and many 2,000-year-old Sequoias (redwoods), most of our region's Douglas fir is in the range of 400 years old. A few 800-year-old giants remain, but they never dominated the landscape.

"The Sequoia is a climax forest species, meaning that it can perpetuate itself one tree at a time for eons. New seedlings can actually sprout from stumps or downed logs. Not so with the shade- intolerant Douglas fir, which must dominate its landscape in order to perpetuate itself.

"Nature has perpetuated Douglas fir as a species by clearcutting, with fire, wind, disease, and yes, even volcanic eruptions. These great natural disasters, which have been scientifically and historically documented, gave each succeeding Douglas fir forest the foothold it needed, until today the species dominates the forests of the Pacific Northwest.

"Although the ecology of Douglas fir forests is well known to every student of forestry, its science has not prevented the Audubon Society and other preservationist groups from nurturing the notion that Douglas fir forests are indeed ancient, or that we must preserve more than the 3.2 million acres of old growth that have already been reserved in the national forests of Oregon and Washington.

"The earliest beginnings of the Society drumbeat may have emerged in the March 1986 edition of *Audubon* magazine, with writer David Kelly tracing the slow emergence of an old-growth Douglas fir grove from the present-day Willamette National Forest.

"'By the time Columbus made landfall in the New World, the new Douglas fir grove was higher than a man's head,' Kelly wrote. 'And for the next century it grew rapidly, a characteristic that would not be lost on men of a much later age. It was a mature forest again before the death of Sir Walter Raleigh in 1618. Overmature, a modern commercial forester would have thought, overdue for the ax.'

"Kelly's article, titled "The Decadent Forest " lays out the Society's strategy for using the northern spotted owl as a surrogate for blocking the harvest of old-growth Douglas fir; a strategy made necessary by the fact that Congress has made no special provision for preserving old-growth forests, except as a wilderness resource, or in other set-asides deemed necessary to protect scenic vistas, wildlife habitat, soil or water quality. Of the 6.2 million acres of Oregon and Washington old growth the Forest Service counts, 3.2 million acres fall under these various no-harvest classifications. The remaining 3 million acres do not, and are the subject of the ancient forest harvest debate. The Society is pinning its hopes and its legal strategy on Federal laws that protect the habitat of endangered plant and animal species.

"'The northern spotted owl is the only species whose survival has been proven to depend on old growth,' Kelly wrote of the Society's desire to link the owl's survival to its old-growth campaign.

"However, the Society's contention that spotted owls *need* old-growth habitat to survive remains a question mark with wildlife biologists who think it may be possible to provide for the bird's habitat needs without setting aside the region's entire old-growth reserve. (See Larry Irwin, below)

"Nevertheless, the Society has moved ahead on the political front, forging a powerful new alliance with the Wilderness Society, the National Wildlife Federation and the Sierra Club, all of whom share a desire to block the opening of about 2.4 million acres of roadless forest land west of the Cascades in Oregon and Washington. According to the Forest Service, these roadless areas contain about three million acres of old-growth timber that, barring wilderness designation, would be available for timber harvesting over the next century.

"Recently, the Wilderness Society stepped to the forefront of the debate with release of its white paper, 'End of the Ancient Forests,' in which it forecasts the 'deliberate, institutionalized destruction' of half the region's unprotected old growth within 50 years.

"Though the report goes to considerable length to minimize the economic hardship that would result from banning the harvest of remaining old growth, a much more concise picture of the group's agenda and its view of forestry emerges from the fall 1988 edition of *Wilderness* magazine.

'Roadless areas in our national forests, it should be remembered, are the stuff out of which a lot of designated wilderness is made," writes *Wilderness* editor T.H. Watkins. "If roads are jammed into these regions on a scale that even approaches Forest Service projections, future additions to the National Wilderness Preservation System will be lost forever, as many as 1.5 million acres almost certainly trashed beyond redemption or replanted in stiff, artificial rows of second-growth Douglas fir that forest ecologists deride as cornfields.'

"The new alliance, unveiled Feb. 5 in Portland, will be known as the Ancient Forest Alliance. Its formation signals the escalation of the old-growth debate. The alliance's members--the Audubon Society, the Wilderness Society, the National Wildlife Federation and the Sierra Club--are hoping their collective political clout will catapult the ancient forest debate into the national limelight. Their hopes seem well placed.

"'The fact of national groups getting into the issue is somewhat analogous to the cavalry coming over the hill,' says Andy Kerr, conservation director for the Oregon Natural Resources Council.

"Two issues are driving the escalating old-growth debate. The first is the alliance's view that log exports and modernization of sawmills are causing the loss of many more jobs than will preservation of remaining old growth. (See "The Jobs Equation," below.) The second, as previously noted, is the alliance's use of its own definition of old growth, a definition that has allowed Wilderness Society forest ecologist Peter Morrison to conclude that only 1.1 million acres of unprotected old growth remain in the national forests of Oregon and Washington, not the 5 million acres the Forest Service counts.

"The Forest Service's deputy regional forester for resources, John Lowe, says the Society's charge that the agency has inflated its old-growth estimate by more than 100% is misleading.

"'We're using different definitions (of old growth),' Lowe said in a recent interview. 'We're not arguing with their numbers and we wish they would not argue with ours.'

"It is possible that the argument over definition is a moot point for reasons that are not readily apparent. In a recent article written for the *Oregonian,* retired Forest Service employee Robert Farris, Portland, suggests the Douglas fir is the wrong tree to preserve.

"'There is some confusion between the Douglas fir and the coastal redwood,' Fariss wrote. "Although the two forest types tend to look somewhat alike when seen from the ground, redwood is a climax species. Such a forest can be preserved essentially forever or until geologic conditions change, since redwoods can reproduce themselves; not only can young redwoods grow in shade, but when a tree falls, new trees sprout from the roots of the old tree. Unquestionably, a redwood forest can be preserved for posterity.

"'However,' Fariss concludes, 'if we try to preserve a Douglas fir forest, all that is accomplished is to waste the trees that have been preserved. When a Douglas fir dies and falls, or falls and dies, it will be replaced by other species and the Douglas fir forest will be lost in any event. This does not mean that some old-growth Douglas fir should not be preserved and allowed to die a natural death to demonstrate the nature of Douglas fir, but it may be a question as to how much Douglas fir should be wasted for demonstration purposes.'

"Fariss' perspective is supported, on a limited scale, by the research of Jerry Towle, a 1970s doctoral candidate at the University of Oregon who reconstructed the Willamette Valley landscape of the early 1800s on the basis of information he gleaned from the diaries of early-day homesteaders and scientists, among them Scottish botanist David Douglas, for whom the Douglas fir is named.

"Douglas and others described the valley as 'wild prairie ground gradually rising in the distance into low undulating hills which are destitute of trees, except for scattered oaks.'

"Archeologists were to later determine that the Kalapuya Indians, who inhabited the valley for about 9,000 years, regularly burned the landscape to promote the growth of grasses that attracted deer and elk to their hunting grounds.

"David Keiser, a forester who lives in Medford, traced a similar historic path in a recent editorial published in the Eugene *Register-Guard.* Keiser, who worked in the Siuslaw National Forest in the early 1950s, wrote in response to a letter decrying the harvest of "primeval forests" from the Oregon Coast Range.

"'I'm not sure what 'primeval forests' are,' Keiser wrote, 'but the Coast Range 55 years ago had only a few pockets of old-growth timber, while the vast majority of the forest was 50 to 70 year-old second-growth Douglas fir that seeded the area after a disastrous fire swept the whole Coast Range.'

"Keiser's conclusion, which is founded in Douglas fir's well-documented rebirth by fire or disease is that 'since nature herself did not see fit to 'save the old growth,' it seems a little presumptuous of man to advocate it.'

"These historic and archeological perspectives lend credence to a scholarly report written by Dr. Michael Newton, an Oregon State University forest ecologist who believes it may be possible to replicate the *characteristic appearance* of ancient forests using modern-day forestry techniques.

"'It would be inaccurate to suggest that all of the Douglas fir forests of our region were grasslands,' Newton observes. 'But there is much more to old growth than the definitions imply. For example, there are managed second growth stands here in Oregon that actually meet the ecological definition of old growth.'

"Newton confesses deep concern over the direction in which the old growth debate is drifting.

"'It is wrong to project the notion that our Douglas fir forests are like the Sequoias which have been with us from 2,000 to 2,500 years,' he says. 'We cannot preserve Douglas fir in the same manner as we have preserved Sequoias and Redwoods, no matter how many laws we pass in the name of protection. Nature makes no allowance for preserving Douglas fir. It does not replace itself except by catastrophe in the form of wind, fire or disease. We have only one choice where our Douglas fir forests are concerned. We can harvest and replant them, or eventually they will be replaced by the inevitable forces of nature.'

Newton ends his discourse on a disquieting note.

"'When old growth Douglas fir dies off, an acre or a tree at a time, the vegetation that grows back is not Douglas fir. It may be hemlock, spruce, cedar or perhaps even brush. I know of 400-year-old brush fields here in Oregon that have grown up where forests once stood. Let's just say that the ecological story I see in Oregon's forests is quite different from the popularly reported version you find in magazines and newspapers.' [107]

In retrospect, the essay by Reinhart is a fair representation of the conflict between those who wish to use the forests of the Pacific Northwest for multiple uses and values and those who wish to lock up the national forests and try to preserve the forests in a state undisturbed by man.

Many assumptions underlie the arguments on both sides. In the same issue of *EVERGREEN* a wildlife biologist, Larry L. Irwin, is interviewed about the validity of using the northern spotted owl as a surrogate via the Endangered Species Act to halt the cutting of older or all forests in national forests. The National Council for Air and Stream Improvement (NCASI) is the environmental research arm of the forest products industry. It was formed in the 1940s to perform independent, scientific assessment of environmental questions associated with the industry. NCASI guards carefully its independence and its reputation for quality scientific research. The report on the Dr. Irwin's interview was thus:

"In Dr. Larry Irwin's work, the only constant is change. Irwin directs a wildlife research program for the National Council for Air and Stream Improvement (NCASI).

"As project leader for the Corvallis-based wildlife program Irwin is one of a handful of scientists seeking to define the habitat needs of the northern spotted owl.

"Although too little is known about the owl, wildlife biologists now believe that owls nest most frequently in old-growth timber stands. What remains a mystery is how much old-growth timber a pair of nesting owls requires to ensure the survival of their young.

"Preservationist groups, anxious to bring a halt to old-growth timber harvesting in the region's publicly-owned forests, have taken the position that spotted owls are totally dependent on old-growth habitat and that, as a result of this, all old-growth timber harvesting must be stopped before the owl perishes.

"The timber industry, which is heavily dependent on publicly-owned timber supplies, which include old growth, has taken the opposite view, noting that continuing owl research has turned up many more owls than were thought to exist and that owls are, with increasing frequency, found in young stands of timber.

"Irwin, who is a soft-spoken man, has wisely distanced himself from this debate, so as to preserve the integrity of his research.

"'The environmental point has been made,' Irwin says of the litany of lawsuits and timber sale appeals filed by the Audubon Society, the Wilderness Society and the Sierra Club Legal Defense Fund. 'Now it is time for us to begin to address the problems that researchers have identified.'

"Ironically, it may be that the biggest problem with spotted owl research is that the right questions aren't being asked.

"'For too long, we've been asking ourselves a lot of impact-related questions concerning the relationship between timber harvesting and the owl,' Irwin says. 'We've ignored the most important question of all, which is 'What is the feasibility for managing wildlife species, like the owl, that we think find optimal habitat conditions in old-growth forests?' Asking this question will lead us to development of a broad-based 'how-to' knowledge base which will be far more useful and far more beneficial to the owl than the problem-related knowledge base we have now."

"Irwin, who holds masters and doctoral degrees in wildlife management, believes it may be possible to accommodate both owls and loggers in the forests of the Pacific Northwest through better integration of timber and wildlife management plans.

"'There are some very heavy scientific questions to be answered,' Irwin acknowledges, 'but there are many examples of the success of this kind of integration.'

"One such example involves wild turkeys that, for years, were thought to require at least 5,000 acres of undisturbed bottomland hardwood as nesting habitat. Today, as a result of the kind of effort Irwin envisions, turkeys are relatively numerous in intensively managed upland pine stands.

Could it happen this way with the spotted owl?

"'We can be hopeful for this,' Irwin says, 'but there are a lot of 'how to' questions we need to answer first.'

"One of the most difficult challenges Irwin faces results from the tremendous diversity of forests here in the Pacific Northwest.

"'The forests of eastern Washington are much different from the forests of western Oregon,' Irwin explains. 'We need to understand how wildlife species adapt to this natural diversity before we can fully understand how they adapt to man's presence.'

"Irwin acknowledges that 'only a handful' of the 400 or so vertebrate species living in Pacific Northwest forests have actually had difficulty adapting to the presence of man.

"'Most wildlife species adapt quickly to timber harvesting-related activities,' Irwin says. 'In fact, some species, like deer and elk, have enjoyed considerable food chain benefit as a result of timber harvesting. But a few species, like the owl, may have difficulty until we learn how to integrate timber and wildlife management schemes.'

"Irwin is more optimistic about the outcome of his research than he was two years ago.

"'We've come a long way, scientifically and philosophically,' he observes. 'The public forest management agencies and the timber industry have shown great interest in funding cooperative research necessary to answer the questions we need to be asking about the owl's habitat requirements.'"[108]

In the same March/April 1989 issue of *Evergreen* an article by the editor, Jim Peterson, addressed the question of the cause/effect relations between old-growth availability for harvest and jobs.   Recall that environmentalists had been presenting the case that it was log exports and increased mill efficiency and not timber availability that were causing layoffs in the timber industry. The article, "The Jobs Equation: What's Really Behind the Mill Closures," had this to report:

"It does not take a rocket scientist to figure out what is causing mill closures and shift curtailments in Southwest Oregon's forest products industry.

"At least not according to Dr. Con Schallau, a research economist with the U.S. Forest Service Pacific Northwest Station at Corvallis.

"'The log supply is drying up,' Schallau says flatly. 'Mills can't operate without logs. It is hard for me to understand how anyone could dispute this. The arithmetic is very simple. '

"When attorneys representing the Northwest Forest Resources Council petitioned the Ninth Circuit Court of Appeals requesting that it lift its injunction blocking the harvest of old-growth timber from O&C forest lands in western Oregon, they presented several sworn statements, including one from Gov. Neil Goldschmidt which blamed the log shortage on the BLM spotted owl lawsuit filed by several preservationist groups.

"'The injunction has caused significant dislocation in the supply of raw materials to these (affected) companies and their mills and has led to layoffs and mill closures, ' Goldschmidt said in his sworn statement to the court.

"But preservationist groups who filed the BLM spotted owl lawsuit continue to argue that mill closures and job losses are the result of raw log exports and continued automation of sawmills. In fact, they were so outraged by the court's decision to lift its injunction that they announced they would seek sanctions against NFRC attorney Mark Rutzick for 'lying' to the court.

"The log export issue has been hotly debated in Oregon and Washington.

"Recently the Southern Oregon Timber Industries' Association, Medford, and Douglas Timber Operators, Roseburg, took an unprecedented step into the debate by announcing that their 200-plus member companies oppose the export of raw logs from public forest lands.

"'None of the 137 members of our association export raw logs,' reports SOTIA executive vice president, Greg Miller. 'But there is a public perception that mill closures in Southwest Oregon are somehow related to log exporting. In truth, log exporting under current federal export laws is a non-issue in Southern Oregon because most of our timber comes from federal lands, and federal law prohibits the export of raw logs from lands managed by the Forest Service and the Bureau of Land Management.'

"DTO executive director, Troy Reinhart, echoed Miller's statement, adding that mill closures and shift curtailments in Southwest Oregon are the result of reductions in harvest levels on national forests, declining congressional appropriations for timber management, and the BLM spotted owl lawsuit.

"'One-third of the BLM's timber sale program could be lost as a result of this one lawsuit,' Reinhart said. 'More than 600 Southwest Oregon mill workers are on reduced work schedules, or have lost their jobs altogether because their companies cannot find the logs they need to keep operating.

If we lose this court case, more than 6,000 people working in Southwest Oregon communities will lose their jobs.'

"Reinhart bases his forecast on Forest Service research which shows that each million board feet of timber harvested in Southwest Oregon generates eight industry jobs, and that each industry job creates two additional service sector jobs.

"'The arithmetic is pretty simple,' Reinhart says. 'It shows 2,500 jobs lost from the BLM's Roseburg District, 1,500 jobs lost from the Medford District, and 1,268 jobs lost from the Coos Bay District.'

"Preservation groups, anxious to distance themselves from the specter of unemployed workers, dispute Reinhart's claim, noting that automation of sawmills and plywood manufacturing facilities is causing far greater job losses than the BLM spotted owl lawsuit.

"Schallau disagrees.

"'There is much more to this jobs and automation question than simplistic discussions can reveal,' he begins. 'A tight supply of public timber forced processors to bid up stumpage prices to unprecedented levels prior to 1979. The ensuing collapse of the building industry caught many operators with timber they could not afford to harvest and process. The subsequent national recession made the situation worse and many mills closed, some permanently.' Schallau acknowledges that automation has cost some workers their jobs but, he adds, 'the shortage of logs at the end of the 1970s, and now, is contributing to the decision to install labor-saving technologies.'

"'Improvement of existing manufacturing capacity, through installation of new technology is an ongoing thing,' Schallau concludes. 'Normally this can be accommodated by local economies, but not when log supplies are cut back on the scale currently being experienced.' In Schallau's opinion, automation has enabled Oregon's forest products industry to remain competitive in very competitive domestic and international markets for finished products. He does not believe the industry would be in business in Oregon today if it had not had the foresight to invest in labor saving processes.

"'Its ironic,' Schallau continued. 'The timber industry is seen as a culprit for having automated, while other industries, most notably steel and automobiles, are criticized for the massive layoffs that resulted from their not having the foresight to invest in technologies that would have allowed them to maintain the competitive edge they held from the beginning of the industrial age.'

"Economists do not dispute the fact that automation has caused job displacement in Oregon's forest products industry.

"Gary Lettman, a forest economist with the Oregon State Department of Forestry, reports that, since 1955, the number of workers needed to manufacture one million board feet of lumber or 1 million square feet of plywood has dropped from five to two.

"'But,' Lettman argues, 'mill modernization has been a plus for Oregon because it has enabled the industry to improve product quality and, at the same time, reduce labor costs. As a result, Oregon's forest products are in high demand.'

"The national recession of the early 1980s dealt a devastating blow to forest industry employment. It plummeted from a record 81,000 jobs in the late 1970s to a low of 56,000 in 1982. Since then, it has rebounded to 68,000 jobs, leaving no doubt in Schallau's mind that the recovery of the forest products industry led Oregon out of the recession.

"'No serious economist can dispute this fact,' he said in a 1988 interview in *Forest Life*.

"Still, Lettman expects the trend toward increased efficiency through automation to continue.

"'Automation in the forest products sector was predicted before the recession,' he says. 'The recession allowed the streamlining to proceed at a faster pace than had been forecast.'

"Writing in *Assessment of Oregon's Forests*, a recently released department of forestry publication, Lettman made this prediction.

"'More than half the timber harvested in Oregon is sold at public auction. Competition for this timber will intensify because timber availability is expected to decrease dramatically on industrial forest lands. Therefore, the only major costs of production under control of the forest industry are capital, labor costs and raw material waste. The forest industry has and can be expected to continue to increase utilization of raw materials, capital and labor with a vengeance.'

"Automation has not, in Lettman's view, reduced rural Oregon's historic dependence on forest products employment.

"'Oregon's basic economy is still heavily dependent on the wood products industry,' Lettman writes. 'Thirty-eight percent of Oregon's private basic employment is generated in this sector. Most heavily dependent upon the wood products industry is Southwest Oregon. Coos, Curry, Douglas, Klamath and Lake Counties are all more than 70 percent dependent upon the lumber and wood products industry for generation of private outside income. Jackson and Josephine Counties as well as West-central, Central and Northeast Oregon are all more than 50 percent dependent.'

"Schallau's research underscores Lettman's analysis. He notes that 41 percent of all value-added manufacturing in Oregon in 1986 was in the forest products sector.   By contrast, 15 percent was in agriculture and 5 percent was in high technology.

"Indeed, it appears that value-added manufacturing is one of the bright spots on the wood products employment horizon. Lettman reports employment in this sector, sometimes called 'secondary manufacturing,' has doubled since 1982, thus softening the impact of job losses caused by automation. In rural Crook County, 1986 industry employment actually exceeded 1979s state record level, the result of a rapidly expanding door and window cut-stock industry.

"'The untold story here concerns the number of jobs created by new manufacturing technologies,' Schallau says. 'These technologies have created jobs manufacturing wood-based products that didn't even exist 10 years ago. I do not want to imply that there has been a one-for one tradeoff in employment, but what we do have is a very competitive, technologically superior industry that is well positioned to take advantage of growing demand for the products it manufactures.'

"Lettman and Schallau agreed that the bottom line is timber supply. In their opinion, it supersedes all other issues, including the human impact of automation.

"'Oregon's economy is diversifying,' Lettman writes. 'Decade by decade, it has become less dependent upon the wood products industry, and this trend is expected to continue. Therefore, it is of the utmost importance that planning by public ownerships provide adequate stumpage supplies while Oregon is making the transition to a more diversified economy.'

"Schallau agrees, but traces a more troubling perspective he sees on the horizon. He points to a recent *Journal of Forestry* article by Perry Hagenstein, a Massachusetts resource economist who predicts that '. . a continuation of restrictive public timber-harvest policies during the 1980s and 1990s would shift about $4 billion of income annually from timber consumers (individual consumers of forest products and the timber processing industry) to public and other timber owners in the Northwest.'

"Furthermore, Schallau says, 'as wood costs increase because of log shortages, more environmentally inferior wood substitutes, such as plastics, steel and aluminum, will be consumed.'

"Schallau's conclusion.

"'It just doesn't make sense, from economic or environmental perspectives, for society to allow this to happen when wood-based products can meet so many of our needs without causing the kind of mass dislocation that is being forecast.'"

Many years earlier Niclaos Rashevsky described how complex systems could shift to unexpected states when changes were too fast or too slow, that is, abnormal to the system.[109] Here in a socio-economic setting we see two thoughtful people arguing for making change slowly in a complex biosocial system.

But things may not always change slowly. On April 26, 1989, the U. S. Fish and Wildlife Service announced that, "(T) hey found that the northern spotted owl warrant Federal protection as 'threatened' species because of significant modification and loss of its forest habitat."[110]

CHAPTER SEVEN

May 1989

By early summer, 1989, a sense of urgency filled the air. The USFWS had published in the Federal Register its intent to list the NSO. Listing would impact timber harvest on federal land, which would result in greatly reduced harvest levels. These lower levels would impact local governments and people. Feelings—anger, hope despair, compromise—ran to highs or lows.

The Northwest Forest Resource Council published information on the NSO-Timber situation. The Council was an association of several timber organizations in the Pacific Northwest. These organizations kept track of federal timber sales for the region. By the time the paper was published clear trends were apparent. One way of showing the trend is to trace the amount of timber under contract on the national forest and BLM districts in the region, by quarter. In the first quarter of 1985, the total for both agencies was just over 22 billion board feet; in the last quarter of 1988 the total was just over nine billion board feet, more than a 50 percent reduction.[111] While the amount of timber was steadily declining, the money that counties received in a given year varied depending on the overall economy. The data below,[112] in millions of dollars, shows clearly the recession in the early 1980s and the recovery that had occurred by 1988.

DISTRIBUTIONS TO COUNTIES IN OREGON

YEAR	USFS $	BLM $	TOTAL $
1978	101.6	96.8	198.4
1979	121.0	97.6	218.6
1980	98.9	97.0	195.9
1981	95.0	39.3	134.3
1982	46.8	47.8	94.6
1983	69.2	47.8	117.0
1984	86.5	117.5	204.0
1985	94.6	10.2	104.8
1986	117.1	72.4	189.5
1987	131.9	69.3	201.2
1988	144.5	108.3	252.8

The impact of these dollars on school districts, for example, is more obvious if we look at the dollars per child received in a district for a year from timber harvest. For the 1986-1987 school year it varied from a low of less than a dollar per child, in Portland, to a high of over $3190, in Andrews

School District, Harney County. The mean distribution per child was $186.17; the median was $49.50.[113] For Rep. Van Leeuwen, the more significant figures were those for Linn County. The average payment in 1986-87 for Linn County schools was $115.70 per child, for a total of $1.85 million to county schools of a total of $9.22 million distributed to the county in fiscal 1986.

History showed clearly that with reduced timber harvests on the national forests would substantially reduce operating expense money for the district and the people she served.

The press was making an effort to get a dialogue going. Discussions between an industry representative and an environmental representative that were held at a timber sale site on the Willamette National Forest were reported by a team from the Albany *Democrat Herald.*[114] A sidebar quote from Jim James, a participant in the discussion, summarized the article: "I think what we agree on is that we need to be prudent managers of our forest land. What we disagree on is the definition of prudent timber management."

The supervisor of the Willamette National Forest joined the fray. He pledged that the U S Forest Service would seek all reasonable means to achieve a harmonious balance between owls and timber. He reminded his readers that the Forest Service's mission is to "Care for the land and serve people."[115] A letter writer to the Lebanon paper called it a bitter pill to swallow when she learned that her contributions to National Wildlife Foundation and the Audubon Society were being used to bring lawsuits to halt timber harvest.[116]

The poignant story of one man's experience, really his survival battle, exposed the pain felt in places where timber harvest had been reduced and then recovered, to some degree. Robert Heilman wrote,

"I used to work for a white-haired, old gyppo logger who taught me many things about living and working around here. I remember one morning when he told me about the recession of 1958. We were taking a coffee break in the little two-man sawmill he'd built with discarded equipment and old-truck parts. As he talked, we watched a bird building her nest in the rafters of the mill shed.

"It was 1958 and timber industry wages and per capita income levels in Douglas County were at an all-time high. 'They used to call them panics,' he said, 'and then it was depressions, and nowadays they call them recessions, but it's all the same thing. Every time things get rolling good, to where there's lots of small outfits working, money gets tight and the bottom falls out of everything. Then, after the smoke clears, you look around and most all the little guys are gone and the big outfits are bigger than ever.'

That particular slump, back in '58, had cost him his home and his sawmill. He went to work in Northern California as head sawyer and then supervisor of someone else's mill. He stayed a few years, long enough to gather up a grub stake and return home to begin again. 'A man does what he has to do to get by,' he said.

"In 1982, I bought a Brown Swiss milk cow and raised a small flock of laying hens. The unemployment rate that year averaged 17.2 percent in our county.

"The cow gave four gallons of milk every day and the hens laid about a dozen eggs. I began selling eggs and milk to my friends at cost. I let them have the food on credit and allowed them to pay with barter (poached venison on one occasion) or with food stamps when they didn't have the money.

"Poor people break laws as a matter of survival; corporations break laws as a matter of business acumen. Like many of my neighbors (and all of my friends) I lived as the pettiest sort of criminal—driving without car insurance; selling raw, uninspected milk; accepting food stamps without authorization; eating poached fish and game.

"It is not something I am proud of nor particularly ashamed of, either. Pride and shame were luxuries we couldn't afford at the time. Sometimes the jug of milk and carton of eggs I dropped off was all that a family had to eat. Somehow there was always enough cash for a bale of alfalfa hay or a sack of grain when I needed it.

"By the fall of 1985, unemployment had dropped to 11.6 percent with the long-awaited trickle-down. By then most of the families who were my customers and friends were gone. There weren't enough of them left in the valley to cover the cow's feed costs. I gave up my one-man, one-cow, non-profit dairy and sold her at auction.

"Bit by bit, we lost our self-respect as we knocked up against hard realities and even harder institutions that were indifferent to our humanity. It was a slow process, one that we feared but couldn't really see happening.

"It's hard to wait when you are used to working. There's a slow, steady erosion that wears down a few people first, and then whole families crumble like dirt clods running through your fingers. Finally, the community itself is gone, washed down river, never to return. 'And I alone am escaped to tell thee.'

"Davey was my neighbor's son when we lived in town. He and I worked on the same tree-planting crew for a local mill during the winter of 1976. In the spring of that year he got a job in the mill. He was 18, fresh out of high school, earning $5.35 an hour.

"In the spring of 1986, I ran into him in the grocery store. He'd been out of work for nearly a year but had just landed a job in another mill. He

69

was grateful to have found work, which I could understand since he was now 28, married and a father.

"'Well, that's good to hear,' I congratulated him. 'How much are you making?'

"'$4.75 and hour.'

"I should have kept my mouth shut. But a little mental arithmetic told me that, given the inflation rate, he was earning about half the pay he had as a raw kid.

"Jeeze! You guys are still eligible for food stamps.

"He looked away, over at the stacked boxes of margarine before he spoke.

"'Yeah, well, actually I'm getting more than most of the guys because I've got experience. Starting pay's $4.00 an hour.'

"It's been an odd sort of recovery. Timber harvest levels for Douglas County were 400 million board feet higher in 1986 than in 1978, but produced $55 million less in wages. While the timber industry has become 'leaner, more productive and cost effective.' The people have simply become leaner.

"In 1988, the sixth straight year of economic recovery brought one in six Umpquans in for emergency food boxes or meals. Local relief agencies estimate less than 5,000 pounds of emergency food were distributed in Douglas County in 1978. Today the 93,000 people living in the Umpqua eat nearly a million pounds of emergency food every year."[117]

Ten years later with the benefit of 20/20 hindsight it is very clear what was happening in the timber-dependent communities. The federal agencies were trying to help maintain viable communities; environmentalists were bent on stopping timber harvest; companies were looking at the bottom line. The people in the communities were being starved out. Just as every animal in the forest will fight back if cornered, the people in the communities in the forests fought back, too.

"Big trucks carry timber workers' protest on spotted-owl issue through Hood River."[118] blared the headline. The sub-heading said, "Loggers and millworkers and their families say they will be the victims if the bird is declared threatened." A picture accompanied the article showing a woman holding a sign that said, "Save Our Jobs!"

The national media were trying to tell the story of what was going on in the spring of 1989 in the timber towns of the west. One attempt was by Peter Jennings on ABC on April 26, 1989. Shortly thereafter Marian Nelson, of Sweet Home, OR, wrote to Mr. Jennings. Her letter was published in the local paper. She said in part:

"I was deeply disappointed to hear of your extremely biased and basically untrue story, concerning the timber industry and old growth timber...

"I would invite you to do your research with some actual experts in the field, not hired environmentalists who are paid to put spikes in trees and chain themselves up...

.

.

"We still have many thousands of acres of standing timber in the state of Oregon. It is not a devastated wasteland as portrayed on your news program. Mr. Jennings 'YOU HAVE BEEN HAD' by a dedicated, rich group of people who have no qualms about totally devastating our beautiful state..."[119]

The irony of all this was obvious to a careful observer. The U. S. Forest Service had launched its Spotted Owl Research, Development and Application program on April 5, 1989[120]. The Program had these goals:

"Specific goals of the Program include providing *preliminary* (emphasis added) information on the abundance and distribution, reproductive ecology, and habitat requirements of the spotted owl; coordinating a monitoring and inventorying program on National Forests to gather information on the status of spotted owl areas and populations; and providing guidelines for managing forests to insure viable populations of spotted owl."

The U. S. Fish and Wildlife Service later, On April 26, 1989, based its listing as threatened for the spotted owl on the "significant modification and loss of its forest habitat." Yet, about three weeks earlier the U. S. Forest Service had announced its program to get preliminary information on the critical subjects that were assumed as truth in the listing announcement. Twenty five million dollars were to be spent over the next five years.

For a seasoned state legislator with a lifetime of farm experience it must have been shocking to see correlation used to establish a cause/effect relation. Mature forest was being harvested; hence owls must be in trouble. But the U. S. Forest Service was just beginning to get preliminary information.

Rather than continue to cut old growth, someone suggested that the younger forests could be thinned. A story with a Eugene, OR, dateline reported that efforts would be made to do that. The U. S. Forest Service had told local congressmen that it would need $6 million to prepare the sales. U. S. Reps. Peter DeFazio and Les AuCoin promised to urge Congress to provide the money. "When you're staring unemployment in the face, any timber is better than none," DeFazio said.[121]

The next day, May 6, 1989, the Albany *Democrat Herald* used its editorial page to explain the crux of the problem the listing of the owl would have on the rural communities in Oregon. The editorial said:

"'Nobody really knows.' That's the answer to the question of how many jobs Oregon will lose as the result of measures to protect the spotted owl.

"But you don't have to know the exact number of jobs being lost to realize that the impact on some people and communities could be devastating.

"'Shortage of timber 'not catastrophic,' the Register Guard in Eugene said in a banner headline on a story out of Salem, reporting on job-loss estimates by the Governor's Council of Economic Advisers.

"Whether it's 'catastrophic' or not depends entirely on whether your job is the one that get wiped out, or whether it's your community that suffers the consequences of unemployment and business decline.

"The state economist, Ann Hanus, guessed that about 6,100 timber-industry jobs would be lost within one year if the federal court injunctions against logging old trees on the federal forests stay in effect. A few of those jobs might come back the second year, according to her forecast, and the net loss in the industry then would be about 5,300. Those losses would ripple through the rest of the economy. According to the state's economic model, one other job would evaporate for every timber-industry job that is lost. So the total losses after one year might be around 12,000.

"In a state with more than 1 million people working, a loss of 12,000 jobs doesn't amount to much—not until you realize that the losses will not be evenly distributed. Instead, the losses will hit mainly the timber-dependent towns and counties of western Oregon. Some of those places only have a few hundred jobs each, and losing many of them could wipe them out.

"In Portland, Salem and Eugene, where mills are not the bedrock of the economy, the loss of a few hundred mill jobs may not sound like a big deal. 'Let them retrain for other jobs,' is the usual refrain. The people who say this usually don't have the slightest idea of what it means to 'retrain.' And the advice is especially galling when it comes from senior people on the public payroll, whose livelihood is assured.

"All the talk about the number of jobs lost hides the fact that every single family-supporting job that disappears causes a great deal of hardship—hardship that politicians and federal judges rarely hear about and never experience first-hand.

"So even if the timber crisis doesn't kill off the entire Oregon economy, it's still a disaster for the adults and children whom it hits, and the towns where they live."[122]

That theme—the people and communities hurt by cut backs in federal timber availability might be few in number, but they were really hurting and had few alternatives—could be heard over and over again. Somehow this impact on real people in real communities had no apparent impact on those seeking the halt of timber harvest on federal land. The headline "Environmentalists seek logging bans," with the sub-heading, "They are appealing numerous timber sales in addition to the 165 sales that are blocked by spotted owl suits," appeared over a story that told of the efforts of groups such as Oregon Natural Resource Council, Headwaters and Siuslaw Task Force to stop logging federal land.[123]

Efforts by a national television network and the largest newspaper in the state to paint a picture of the forestry situation in Oregon and the Pacific Northwest tended to establish as truth fallacies that were not immediately obvious to viewers and readers. Other newspapers, as we saw above in the *Democrat Herald* editorial, such as the Sweet Home *The New Era*, tried valiantly to dispel the fallacies. In an opinion piece *The New Era* had this to say under a heading "Separating fact from fallacy":

"Fallacy: Oregon is raping the nation's forests.

"Fact: Over 100 million seedlings are planted each year in Oregon alone. That's 37 seedlings per Oregonian or 1.2 seedlings per person on a national average.

"Fallacy: The last old growth tree stands alone atop the Cascade Mountains, as a chainsaw-weilding logger chomps at the bit waiting to fall it...

"Fact: Nearly 3.5 million acres of trees have been set aside in long term sustained yield management programs.

"Fallacy: Millions of acres of trees are being cut each year and no new trees are being planted...

"Fact: In Oregon alone in the 1988-89 planting year, some 200,000 acres were replanted with 100 million seedlings. Since 1960, yearly seedling plantings have risen from 60 million to a high of 110 million in 1980.

"The list of fallacies could go on and on and on...the problem is that far too many Americans view those fallacies as truths delivered in bite-size portions by the national media during breakfast, dinner and supper news breaks."

To the residents of a federal timber dependent town, developments seemed overwhelming. Mary Brady, of Sweet Home, wrote to the editor expressing her concern about developments in timber supply and the NSO.[124] She told how she lived in a house made of wood and wondered where the environmentalists lived. She said she heated her house with wood and wondered where the environmentalists thought the wood came from in the fires at their protest sites. She said she used paper that was made of wood and supposed that the legal documents on which the environmentalists made their case were also written on paper. And finally, she wrote that members of her family paid taxes that supported welfare and supposed that Earth First! members used welfare to support themselves, or maybe they could provide support of the out-of-work timber workers.

In early May 1989, it was not clear how many jobs would be eliminated in order to save the NSO. As one reporter put it, "The figure depends on who is doing the figuring."[125] The figures varied from 41,000 according to some estimates down to, "There is an impact, but that impact is small," according to the president of the Oregon Natural Resources Council Board.

One commentator, Russell Sadler, said in a speech near Ashland, OR that the real issue was timber supply, not the owl or old growth.[126]

Whatever the real issue, efforts were being made to get some resolution to the problem of timber harvest on federal land. A Spotted Owl summit was being discussed for June 24, 1989 in Portland. Politicians and interested parties hoped some agreement could be reached.[127]

It seemed that almost every issue of every newspaper had some sort of an article or comment about the spotted owl issue. An example was an Op-Ed piece by Sandra Schukar in the *Statesman Journal.*[128] Ms. Schukar, whose family was in the logging business, said, "Several of us directly involved in the timber industry have been 'too busy' trying to earn a decent living to bother to express our opinion. I personally would like to see us concentrate on saving the timber industry and the rest of Oregon's economy." This came after a listing of the people her company supported and the importance of their relatively small payroll to the overall economy.

A letter to the editor discussed some misconceptions regarding the Endangered Species Act and the NSO, and concluded by saying, "Let us have responsible discussion of the law and the scientific data among all interested parties. Then perhaps we can make some informed decisions."[129]

There would be reductions in timber harvest. BLM's harvest would be a third less than average.[130] This was due to continued restrictions on logging northern spotted owl-nesting sites. The effect of this reduction on timber dependent communities was vividly portrayed in a letter from Edith M. Darling, Lebanon, OR, to the editor. After describing the nature of a timber dependent town and the importance of timber jobs to all in the community, she put this slant on the impact of lost timber jobs:

"Every time an Oregonian loses his or her job in the timber industry, his or her family is totally deprived of income. These families include children. Through no fault of the parents, these children are being deprived of food, clothing and shelter. This deprivation could result, directly or indirectly, in the death of many of these children. This is child abuse of the worst kind!"[131]

This people versus owl discussion was one that was often held at the time. In fact, it continues to the present day. Nevertheless, attempts were being made to work out a compromise. In a story from Washington, DC it was reported that the BLM and US Forest Service were trying to devise a solution that would save some timber jobs and the owl at the same time.[132] Senators and Representatives from the West were actively involved in the discussions.

Rep. VanLeeuwen put together a fact sheet and sent it to constituents.[133] In a covering note she said, "We have been bombarded with figures in the past months, some of them conflicting, as people have become aware that it is not spotted owls we're talking about; it is the jobs and the livelihood of a whole region that are endangered. In the material to follow, we've tried to sort out what appears to be the most accurate facts. We have also compiled a list of key decision-makers to whom we hope you will write, expressing your concerns and asking for their help."

She listed things she thought Congress should do, facts regarding the timber base, and who owns how much, employment and Wilderness acreages. The information concluded with names and telephone numbers of members of the Executive and Legislative Branches of government, from President George Bush on down.

Whether news was good or not depended on your point of view. Rep. VanLeeuwen with a big, red HOORAY endorsed a report on a ruling by U. S. District Judge Helen Frye that lifted a ban on BLM logging. The story, however, told how Andy Kerr, Oregon Natural Resources Council, had said, "At this point, it appears that Sen. Hatfield's legal shenanigans that placed the BLM above the law has worked." The senator had inserted in a continuing budget resolution an amendment that prohibited challenges to the BLM's timber management plans.[134]

Letters to the editors of mid Willamette valley newspapers played the themes of the argument about timber and owls over and over, each with a different slant on the question. Rintha Renoud, Sweet Home, argued that owls and people should share.[135] The week before Karen Thomas, Albany, suggested that the owls be relocated rather than have timber families displaced.[136] Others asked about how environmentalists lived without wood; another argued that the forest is in a perpetual state of renewal; another blamed all the problems on timber exports.[137]

It did not take long for environmental groups to challenge the ruling of Judge Helen Frye. A report with a San Francisco dateline told of an appeal to the 9th U. S. Circuit Court for an emergency injunction to halt logging of old growth forests within 2.1 miles of spotted owl nests. Oregon Natural

Resources Council, Portland Audubon Society and other conservation groups filed the appeal.[138]

It was a trying time for congressmen from Oregon. Rep. Peter DeFazio reported that he waked some nights in the middle of dreams about ancient forests and lumber mills closing. He said he was spending 70 percent of his time on the timber issue.[139] Senator Mark Hatfield visited with some state legislators and reminded them of the role of federal timber in the State. About $30 million a year comes to school districts in the state from federal timber harvests. He told them, "There is a big group in the mainstream of the environmental community that is not interested in destroying the timber industry." However, it is reported that he said others in the environmental movement, "have said to my face, in plain English language, 'My desire is to freeze the forests of this country and never cut another tree.'"[140]

In an attempt to eliminate the argument about timber exports from the debate Senator Packwood had submitted a bill in Congress that would ban the export of timber from federal forests. With that bill in place he predicted the more difficult task of determining the purpose of the national forests would remain unresolved.[141]

So, as May 1989, came to a close it was apparent to a close observer of the timber industry scene that changes were coming. Log exports from federal land would likely be banned, timber harvests would be reduced unless some accommodation of the owl-timber conflict could be reached, and if timber harvests were reduced, people in the rural communities that depended on timber would be hurt. An editorial reviewing the situation with regard to the owl, timber and people, concluded by saying:

"Because of the time lag between sale and harvest, there's still time for federal authorities to work out a plan to avoid the otherwise sharp reduction in the availability of federal timber. That's why the June 24 timber summit called by state and federal officials is so important. It must result in federal action—by Congress or the forest agencies—to mitigate what otherwise would be a disaster in the Oregon towns that depend on trees."[142]

CHAPTER EIGHT

JUNE FLOWERS—1989

"There are not many forests left to which the spotted owl can flee as the chain saw pursues him into his natural habitat, the last remaining ancient big tree forests in the United States. Already ninety percent of the giant trees that serve as aerie lairs for the owl—some of them seven feet across and hundreds of years old—have fallen before the onslaught of the logger."[143] That is a heart-rending statement. The ninety percent fallen is a figure that comes from the calculation that in the entire United States ninety percent of the forests have been harvested at least once. In the Detroit Ranger District, Willamette National Forest, in the mid-1990s 35 percent of the district had trees over 140 years old; such trees have, therefore, not been exposed to the onslaught of the logger in a district reputed to be the heaviest cut district in a forest reputed to be the heaviest harvested in the national forest system.[144]

The magazine *Oregon Business* reported that the US Forest Service told it that of its 24 million acres of forest in the Northwest, 6.2 million acres were considered old growth—about 25 percent. The Service had plans to log 900,000 acres of that during the next decade and perhaps a total of 2.3 million acres by 2040. That would leave 3.9 million acres of old growth on that date. That is well above the 10 percent claimed to now exist by Humane News.[145]

Earth First!, about which we heard earlier from Dave Foreman, was back in the news. Four members, including Foreman, were arraigned for conspiracy to sabotage nuclear facilities in the Southwest.[146] We shall hear from this group again and again.

The old adage, "Figures don't lie, but liars can figure," often seems appropriate in the timber debate. We have just seen the 10% / 90% figures. An editorial began, "It's hard to imagine a more misleading assertion than this one reported by The Associated Press in one of the stories, printed in our paper, about the timber controversy: 'As the Northwest's economy diversifies and modernizes, wood products have shrunk to 6 percent of Oregon's gross state product and 2.2 percent of Washington's.'" The editorial goes on with the rhetorical question, "It it's true that the timber industry amounts to only 6 percent, why should everybody be so worried?" The answer, it goes on to say, "The key lies in the phrase 'gross state product.'" The editorial explains that gross state product is not the appropriate measure of the importance of the timber industry to the state. It shows that 38 percent of all wage and salary employment in the state of Oregon comes from the timber industry. The editorial concludes: "Basic industries such as these [timber related] have a far greater importance than their proportion of the 'gross state product' would lead people to think."[147]

April showers bring May flowers. By June hope springs eternal in the human breast. In June 1989, it was "New Forestry." " 'I see it as a major philosophical change rather than an incremental change,' said Jerry Franklin, a University of Washington professor and U. S. Forest Service scientist who was a leading spokesman for the movement. 'In terms of forestry practice, it is revolutionary.'"[148] In the same article Kathy Johnson, District Ranger, Gold Beach Ranger District, said that, "What we will do is leave the large blocks of old growth forest. As we move out from that large block of old growth forest into areas previously harvested, we feather out the impacts. We'll leave a certain amount of old growth trees per acre. That number increases as you get closer to the undisturbed block of old growth." The article also said that the new practice would result in a 5 percent dip in timber production over the 130-year harvest cycle.

A letter to the editor headed "Students Threatened" took a less sanguine view.[149] The writer, Bruce Thiel, said, "Your Sunday cartoon showing Sen. Bob Packwood standing on a field of tree stumps is unfair both to the senator and the concept of sustained-yield forestry mandated by law. Your cartoon implies that all old-growth trees are about to be cut. This is not true." Continuing, Mr. Thiel said, "Today in Oregon, more than 3 million acres of land are legally off-limits to the chain saws. Thirty-five wilderness areas, seven of which are less than a two-hour drive from Portland, contain 2 million acres of virgin forest. These old-growth lands will remain spotted owl habitat forever." He then wrote, "Instead of the spotted owl, the Oregon schoolchild should be listed as a threatened species. Last year Clackamas County and its schools received $12,741,600. directly from Forest Service and Bureau of Land Management timber sales. Since the injunctions have already curtailed this year's logging, future revenues will decline." Mr. Thiel concluded, "The Fish and Wildlife Status Review has already identified 67 spotted owl sites in timber stands less than 100 years of age. It looks to me as if the owl can adapt. Can the Oregon schoolchild?"

June 24, 1989 was to be a day of reckoning. That was the day of the Timber Summit in Salem. It was a meeting called by the Oregon congressional delegation and Governor Goldschmidt. The purpose of the meeting was, "(T) o obtain, evaluate and clarify information to assist the Oregon congressional delegation and the governor in developing short- and long-term options in resolving timber supply and old growth management conflicts on federal lands in Oregon."[150] The cited article also suggests that while timber interests were receptive to the agenda, environmental groups were less than pleased.

Writers had been predicting that the Timber Summit would be an exercise in futility. For example, *The Oregonian* carried such a piece earlier in the month, before the agenda was announced. The author, William H. Boyer, said,

There are two crucial principles for long-range policies that bear on the solution to the old-growth crisis:

0 One is that the forests must be sustained for present and future generations.

0 The other is that old growth and its ecosystems are essentially non-renewable.[151]

Here, again, we have a judgment being cited as a principle. As we have noted earlier, the forests of the Pacific Northwest are rarely more than 650 years old. It is 10,000 years since the Ice Age. Therefore, the forests have grown, been taken down, and renewed at least 16 times during that period. The old growth is renewable if you are willing to wait 650 years and assure that no fire, insect or disease, pest, or windstorm takes the forest down. Furthermore, as Mr. Thiel reminded readers, there are several million acres of old growth legally set aside for following generations to study and enjoy.

As the Timber Summit approached, several points of view were expressed. Environmentalists wanted more representation on the Summit Panel.[152] The Dean of the Business School, University of Oregon, published an opinion piece in which he argued the importance of the timber industry to Oregon.[153]

The basic information on the amount of volume in what kinds of forests was missing. "Environmentalists see ample timber"[154] was one view of the situation. The same article reported that industry people were saying they couldn't check the statement because they did not know what areas were included in the environmentalists' data. Confusion reigned. On the same day it was reported that the U. S. Forest Service was beginning a survey to find out about the amount of timber and owls.[155] As it turned out, many years would pass and the basic data are still to be determined.

Rep. VanLeeuwen wrote to the new speaker of the House of Representatives in Washington, D. C. She presented her points of view and urged the new speaker to work toward revising the appeals process, assuring sustained yield, and correcting the Endangered Species Act.[156] Over a decade later none of those actions has been taken.

Headlines captured the tenor of the times. "Rosboro to lay off workers," said the Eugene *Register Guard* on June 15, 1989, because of log shortage. The politicians couldn't keep from stepping on each other's toes. The Albany *Democrat Herald* reported on June 16, 1989, "Governor criticizes Packwood's plans for timber meeting." And in a commentary Ron Blankenbaker wrote in the Salem *Statesman Journal* on June 16, 1989, that one explanation of the governor's pushing for the timber summit was to avert attention from his troubles with workers' compensation insurance.

While politicians, environmentalists and timber industry representatives jockeyed for position, things were happening in the woods. A spotted owl was spotted near a timber sale on the Siuslaw National Forest.[157] Timber harvests had been near peak levels on the national forests and BLM lands in 1988. A windfall was due to the counties that had such land.[158] In 1988 Linn County got $7.4 million for county roads and $2.4 million for schools, the article reported. At the same time it was being predicted that mills would have enough timber to keep operating for the summer of 1989.[159]

Some looked for places to place the blame for the owl/timber collection of problems. The National Forest Management Act of 1976 was designed, based on some interpretations, to guide the Forest Service in building relationships with the public through planning. Robert Wolff, a retired federal forester, blamed the forest service for not using the planning process called for in the NMFA to build bridges to the public, thus avoiding the problems the agency faced in 1989.[160]

The Timber Summit was imminent. Nevertheless, other activities had to move forward. In Washington subcommittees were working on budgets. In testimony environmentalists were pleading for reductions in the timber harvest budgets for the Forest Service and BLM. Industry representatives argued that cutting back on harvest levels would bring economic ruin to the region. Congressman AuCoin was said to be preparing "riders" on appropriations bills that would alleviate the problem. [161]

The congressman followed through. He persuaded a House subcommittee to add $17 million to the Forest Service budget so that it could prepare more timber sales in 1990.[162] AuCoin also teamed with Congressman Norman Dicks, D-Washington, to turn back the efforts of Rep. Sidney Yates, D-Illinois, subcommittee chairman, to cut back on timber harvest.[163] However, Yates was joined by two other subcommittee chairmen, Bruce Vento and Harold Volkmer, in his effort to reduce timber harvests and protect old growth. They were saying that the protection is a national issue.[164] If the members of congress were split, so were most Oregonians. *The Oregonian* had conducted a poll of people in the state and found that there was much agreement on banning export of logs from state land, but on other issues there was a nearly even split on timber policies.[165]

On the eve of the Timber Summit, advantage was being sought from all sides. It was reported that Senator Bob Packwood was pressing the environmentalists to give more in the up-coming negotiations because they had more.[166] At the same time those in the woods who wanted to stop timber harvest were active. Tree spiking continued.[167] The article reported on logs that had come from a controversial timber harvest on BLM land in southern Oregon. And federal biologists were moving forward. They proposed threatened status for the northern spotted owl.[168]

The Timber Summit was held as scheduled on June 24, 1989. Compromises of various kinds had been offered. By the following Monday no agreement had been reached. The Chairman, Senator Hatfield, was pressing for agreement so he could get a rider in an appropriations bill. But as the sun went down on the 26th, no agreement had been reached.[169] What had been hammered out was an arrangement whereby there would be reduced timber harvest on federal land of about eight percent in coming fiscal years. One paper suggested that the plan offered some breathing room; it was a morning paper.[170] When the evening editions hit the streets the high hopes for the summit had been dashed.[171] Environmentalists claimed that there was not enough time to study the proposal. Timber industry representatives and members of congress were apparently willing to accept the arrangement, the article reported.

In an election held on the same Tuesday, June 27, 1989, a measure to ban export of logs from state land passed with a more than a 10 to 1 majority.[172]

As June 1989, came to a close, injunctions stopping harvest on federal land were still in place. The effort to reach a compromise had failed, even though some were still trying.[173] Amid uncertainty about what the future held a report from Washington, D. C. must have been a bitter pill for those concerned about the present and future of the timber industry. The chief of the Forest Service reported to a congressional committee, "I don't think we ought to penalize the people of the Northwest, throw people out of work, close down towns, until a biological decision can be made properly." There was a lack of good data to make a decision.[174]

CHAPTER NINE

JULY HEAT—1989

"Sen. Mark O. Hatfield says the 9th U. S. Circuit Court of Appeals is meddling in the management of federal timberlands and he recommends that judicial review of administrative decisions be suspended. "'It's very obvious that the courts, particularly the 9th Circuit Court, are trying to take over the management of public lands,' Hatfield said."[175]

The meeting in late June that was designed to find a compromise solution to the problems surrounding the NSO and timber harvest on federal land had failed to produce a solution acceptable to all. Environmentalists had refused to go along with the deal worked out. Timber interests felt that nothing had changed:

"Update: The timber industry's decision to accept an old growth logging proposal offered by the Oregon congressional delegation at the June 24 summit conference in Salem is not expected to have a significant impact on the region's long-term federal timber supply.

"'Virtually nothing is changed,' say Greg Miller, executive vice president, Oregon Timber Industries Assn., Medford, and Troy Reinhart, executive director, Douglas Timber Operators, Roseburg.

"'The preservationists' refusal to accept the unanimous, bipartisan proposal offered by the Oregon delegation and the governor ought to provide the public with all the evidence it needs concerning the preservationists' total lack of regard for Oregon's timber economy, and for timber families who contribute so mightily to the social and economic well being of our state. Now, more than ever, there is the need for unrelenting political pressure from the grass roots. The public needs to come to grips with the human tragedy that will now unfold as a result of the preservationist rejection of the summit proposal offered by our state's political leaders."[176]

"Loggers See Spotted Owl as a Harbinger of Doom,"[177] read the headline in a major report from Sweet Home, OR by the Los Angeles *Times*. The reporter, Mark A. Stein, had visited Sweet Home. He reported on the dismantling of a timber industry mill, the lay-offs that had occurred and that were expected, the impact on businesses that depend on the timber industry and its employees to stay in business. He attempted to describe the basic argument between preservationists and the people in and out of the timber industry that depend on federal timber for their livelihood. He reported on the anger directed at the owl and the thoughtful responses that showed that the owl itself was not the real problem. Steve

Rood, Dan Conrad and John Kunzman talked with him about the owl bashing and the real problem:

"'We don't really appreciate owl-bashing,' Rood said. 'People who wear T-shirts about fried owls and things—well, it's funny but it's not really what we are about.'

"'The owls are not our enemy,' Kunzman said. The opposition, he and others make clear, are preservationists who have crippled their industry in court.

"'They have their hands around my throat,' Kunzman said.

"'And my throat,' said Conrad, his second-in-command.

"'And the throats of everyone in Sweet Home,' Kunzman added."

Though the USFWS had published in the Federal Register its intent to declare the NSO as threatened, there was still time for comment. One state legislator was suspicious of the science the agency had used to arrive at the proposed listing:

"Cedric Hayden, State Representative District 38, has requested that the U. S. Fish and Wildlife Service allow peer review of its research before any listing of the northern spotted owl as either threatened or endangered.

"'Good science demands it,' he said."[178]

All sorts of people contributed to the discussion about the owl and the industry. In an Op-Ed piece Beverly McVey reported on reading she had done in the Library of Congress in Washington, D. C. She reported on the extensive range of the owl and how it was illogical to list just the northern variant of the owl.[179] In the same issue of the paper the editor reproduced a long commentary on the timber situation that had been published by the Douglas Timber Operators Inc. of Roseburg, OR. That piece examined carefully the issue of people, owls and the forest and said in summary:

"It is clear at this time, that the only lives being threatened are those of the families of the thousands of hard working men and women in the region's timber communities. While long-term answers are sought that will preserve our jobs and our heritage, no owls will die, no 'eco-system' will be endangered! Only our elected officials in our communities, our states, and Congress can undo the mischief of the preservationists and the courts. But it can be done.

.

.

"There is no need to negotiate or compromise our future for the future of our children to satisfy the whims of a few. The forest resources of the northwest can provide it all—clean water, abundant wildlife, recreation, beauty, and the timber to protect our jobs, our communities and the nation's needs for wood products. But only if our elected officials accept those goals. The time has come to stand up and be counted."[180]

Other ways were tried to show the role of the timber industry in the timber dependent town. In Lebanon, the Oregon Project was distributing yellow peel-off dots to attach to currency generated by the timber industry.[181] Sherri Rathsack of Eugene wrote to the editor: "I'd like to invite each preservationist to feel for one moment what the wife of a logger or millworker feels every time she thinks about the future of her family," she wrote. She concluded by saying, "Can you really justify the damage that will be done to my family and the families of thousands of other loggers and millworkers?"[182]

One of the men in Mark A. Stein's story about Sweet Home was the victim of eco-terrorism at his logging site. Several thousands of dollars worth of damage was done to logging equipment.[183] He reported that it would take several days to repair the damage and that his employees would be without work while the repairs were made. At about the same time protesters were blocking a logging operation in southern Oregon.[184]

The failure of the summit to reach a compromise had a negative effect on many. In Eugene a sawmill company gave its employees notice of a 60-day layoff. Politicians were still trying to reach some sort of a solution. Both Senator Hatfield and Senator Packwood continued to press for a solution to the timber problem.[185] That supply and demand were still viable forces in our economy was manifest in a story about bids for timber. Mills were increasing their bids in an effort to have some sort of a timber supply to keep operating, should the impending shortage take place.[186]

It was reported that environmentalists were working "around-the-clock" to offer a counter to the compromise worked out at the timber summit, which they had rejected. The Wilderness Society was the leader of the effort.[187]

At the same time an organization called Communities for a Greater Oregon (CGO) came up with an idea designed to make people in other parts of the United States aware of the plight of timber families in Oregon. They were making plans to invite vacationers from other states to stay with timber families and see for themselves what these families were experiencing and be shown the actual conditions in the forests. Their message was that there were still lots of big trees in Oregon.[188] Representative Peter DeFazio told a Rotary Club that many congressmen from the east just don't understand the situation in Oregon. He gave as an example an encounter with a Connecticut congressman in an elevator. "He said to me, 'I think it's terrible that you're cutting all those trees,' as opposed to being concerned for the 60-90 people that lost their jobs in a Roseburg mill."[189]

Governor Goldschmidt was trying to find a way that would allow the federal agencies to carry out their plans. In mid-July the 9th Circuit Court had restored an injunction barring BLM from logging within 2.1 miles of an owl site. The governor asked his attorney general to file a friend of the court brief asking that the planning process for federal forests be allowed to proceed and be put in place.[190]

The environmentalists presented their proposal for solving the timber crisis in the Northwest. Both the industry and the U. S. Forest Service rejected it. An industry representative said it was the same proposal as had been offered at the summit wrapped in another bundle. The Chief of the Forest Service said the proposal was "unworkable." [191] Meanwhile congress was trying for a solution and timber companies were bending over backward to live with the owl.[192]

Congressmen were continuing to try all ways to forge a solution. U. S. Rep. AuCoin spoke to a group of labor leaders in Portland. His message was that greatly reduced timber harvests would be the result if a compromise on timber harvest were not found.[193]

Dan Kieft, Lebanon, OR did what concerned citizens should do. He looked at the data and wrote to his paper. He found that reports on owls in the 1940s did not mention the spotted owl. Then, in the 1950s, it was identified and reported as rare. He then noted that BLM owls had increased from 204 in 1985 to 488 in 1988. "If this rate of increase continues, there will be major problems with owl overpopulation upsetting the ecological balance within the next few years.[194]

Lawmakers continued to seek a solution. As the end of July 1989 approached, a new proposal, later called the Hatfield-Adams bill, was put forth. It proposed that 10 billion feet of federal timber be sold during the next 14 months. The plan called for avoiding significantly large blocks of old growth to minimize fragmentation. Hatfield touted the bipartisan effort: "We are appealing to the intellect, not the emotions." He estimated the amount to be sold would be about 10 percent less than the amount of timber that would be sold if some sales were not blocked by lawsuits to protect the spotted owl.[195] The U. S. Senate Appropriations Committee approved the compromise. The legislation was in the form of an amendment to the Interior Department spending bill before the committee.[196] The proposal called for selling about 10 billion feet of timber. There were other interesting aspects to the legislation as reported in the Associated Press article by Les Blumenthal, with a Washington, D. C. dateline:

"The proposal also calls for environmentalists to agree to the release of 1.25 billion board feet of the almost 2 billion board feet of timber sales currently enjoined by federal courts in Portland and Seattle.

"If environmentalists and the industry cannot agree to release that volume for sale by Oct. 1, the existing court injunctions would be dissolved legislatively and the Forest Service and BLM, in consultation with the Fish and Wildlife Service and new citizen advisory boards, would decide what timber would be sold.

"The agreement also would prohibit environmentalists from using injunctions to block timber sales in the next fiscal year, which starts Oct. 1."

The full Senate passed the Interior Department appropriation bill despite serious concerns of Vermont's Senator Leahy. Environmentalists promised a floor fight in the House.[197] The timber industry reluctantly supported the compromise.[198] Environmentalists launched a counter attack. They enlisted the ACLU and Union of Concerned Scientists, among others, to help in turning back the Hatfield-Adams amendment.[199]

The month came to a close with two significant actions. It was reported that two lawyers were being investigated by the Oregon State Bar for failing to inform a U. S. District Court of allegedly contradictory scientific information about spotted owls.[200] John Kunzman, president of Communities for Greater Oregon, wrote to the regional director of the U. S. Fish and Wildlife Service asking if the National Environmental Policy Act (NEPA) had been followed by his agency in the spotted owl case. He noted that while the Endangered Species Act did not require an assessment of economic impact of a listing, NEPA required an Environmental Impact Statement of any action by the government that would impact the human environment. He asserted that listing the owl would seriously impact the environment of Sweet Home for the humans in that community if the owl were listed.[201]

1989 was not a peaceful summer in the timber dependent communities of the Pacific Northwest.

CHAPTER TEN

AUGUST 1989

The first half of 1989 had seen hopes for solutions to the spotted owl problems wax and wane. Into this situation Rep. VanLeeuwen injected a sense of reality. She put together a three-page summary of "Timber Related Supply Facts."[202] Such facts tend to get lost in the shuffle of press announcements, public hearings and political posturing. Here is what she wrote under her Oregon House of Representatives letterhead:

TIMBER SUPPLY RELATED FACTS
August 1989
CONGRESS NEEDS TO ADDRESS 3 VITAL ISSUES:

1. Revise the appeals process: All timber sales are monetarily bonded by the timber company awarded the sale. Therefore, people appealing these sales should likewise have to make a similar monetary commitment.

2. Sustained Yield: Congress needs to assure that the Timber Industry has an adequate land base for a sustained yield of timber products and for multiple use purposes. These lands are a strategic national resource which needs to be managed for our nation's secure future and they should be separate from those already set aside for roadless and wilderness areas. Nationwide our economy needs to be assured of a stable Timber Industry.

3. Endangered/Threatened Species Act: There needs to be a better balance in The Endangered/Threatened Species Act so that it cannot be used to destroy local economies.

FACTS INVOLVING AVAILABLE TIMBER BASE:
FOREST AREA IN OREGON:

Of the 62.1 million acres of total land area in Oregon, nearly half, 27.2 million acres, is forested. Of these, 19.8 million acres are capable of growing commercial crops of timber; 11.6 million acres are in Western Oregon.

In Oregon and Washington there are 7.5 million acres of old growth with 4.2 million acres of that old growth in permanent, never to be logged, set asides. 53% of all federal forest land in Oregon and Washington has already been set aside in wilderness or other preserves where timber harvest is permanently forbidden.

FOREST LAND OWNERSHIP IN OREGON
by percentage:

National Forests	48.4%	Industry	23.5%
BLM, Indian	9.5%	Small Private	14.7%
State, local	3.8%		

EMPLOYMENT and ECONOMY:

More than 77,000 Oregonians are employed in lumber and wood products jobs --- two times more workers than in all of the state's new electronics industry.

A total of 18 mills in Oregon have closed (1,485 Family Wage Jobs Lost!), due to the current situation in the Oregon timber industry. There have been announcements of certain closures of 5 more mills by fall (813 fewer jobs!), and possibly of 2 more.15 to 20 percent of Oregon's economy is timber-dependent. Roughly   34% of Oregon's non-public employees are timber dependent. In 16 counties over 50% of the jobs are dependent on the wood and paper products industry.

About 60% of the public timber sales in Oregon & Washington are locked up by court injunctions.   This could directly affect upwards of 16,000 jobs.

In Oregon alone, at least 70 communities are solely or primarily dependent upon the timber industry for their economic base and most depend on public timber for the raw materials for their mills.

Oregon's timber industry accounts for more than 50% of all the new dollars that flow into the Oregon economy each year.

We use thousands of products that come from trees-- electricity, paper of all kinds, rayon, glue extender, shoe heels, railroad ties, cardboard, the list goes on!

Demand for wood products will keep increasing as more of the "baby boomers" reach maturity and want homes of their own.

If the Northern Spotted Owl is listed as a threatened species and the proposed acreages are set aside for each pair, it could well mean the loss of 130,000 jobs in the timber industry and in the retail and service sectors of the economy.

LINN COUNTY WILDERNESS & SET ASIDES:

In Linn County, 40% of the WILLAMETTE NATIONAL FOREST LAND, (188,195 Acres) is locked into wilderness, spotted owl habitat or other types of single use set-asides.   The new management plan now being considered for the next 10 years proposes setting aside even more.

BUREAU OF LAND MANAGEMENT (BLM), manages 88,596 acres of public land in Linn County, most of which is forested. BLM's Santiam Master Unit (SMU), of 94,000 acres, is mostly in Linn County (less than 6,000 acres of the SMU are in Marion County). Right now close to

30% of the BLM unit, or 25,100 acres cannot be harvested because of owl habitat (*14,000 acres), fragile soil (7,300 acres), and riparian zones or streams (3,800 acres). (*There are 5,800 acres of BLM permanently set aside as habitat for 12 pair of spotted owl and an additional 8,200 acres of older growth timber cannot' be harvested due to a court injunction because of 38 more pair of spotted owls.)

If the figures I have been given by the agencies are accurate, that's 213,295 acres --- almost all within Linn County, which cannot be harvested. That's about 2 1/3 acres preserved for every man, woman and child in Linn County!

OREGON WILDERNESS AND SET ASIDES: Oregon has 36 wilderness areas encompassing more than 3,180 square miles (over 2 million acres). A wilderness area is unroaded and undeveloped, there man can enter only by foot, horseback or canoe. Wilderness = 2.1 million acres.

OREGON HAS:

90,000 acres in 225 state parks,
431,326 acres in Forest Service National Recreational areas,
197,850- acres in 4 areas administered by National Parks,
1,829 miles of wild and scenic rivers,
700 Forest Service picnic areas and campgrounds,
97 BLM picnic areas and campgrounds,
35 Wilderness areas with 2.1 m1llion acres,
30 counties with multiple parks,
15 Forest Service geological areas with 21,343 acres,
13 Forest Service scenic areas with 83,981 acres,
7 Forest Service botanical areas - 5,584 acres,
6 Forest Service experimental forest-- 48,730 acres,
5 Forest Service historical areas -- 3,992 acres,
1 National Scenic Area--112,000 acres.

In addition, there are hundreds of miles of hiking trails, 12 ski areas, and 86 other winter sports areas.

REFORESTATION IN OREGON--SUSTAINED YIELD:

In Oregon, during the 1988-89 planting year, an estimated 200,000 acres (i.e.300 square miles) were planted with 100 million seedlings, or 37 seedling trees per Oregon resident.

Oregon's reforestation effort is the largest in the nation. Since 1960, more than one billion seedlings have been planted in the State.

SUPPLY: 18% of all softwood timber growing today in America is in Oregon. In 1988, 20% of all softwood lumber and 40% of all plywood-building panels made in the U.S. were manufactured here in Oregon. Oregon is (or was) the nation's #1 producer of lumber and plywood. Over 50% of the timber for sawmills and plywood plants in Oregon comes from federal forestlands.

IF the "preferred alternatives" of draft forest plans are adopted, the amount of timber available from USFS lands in Oregon will drop at least 20%. (Only 40% of the USFS land will be available for full timber harvest.)
ENVIRONMENT:
Land managers agree that most of Oregon's forests can and do support recreation, wildlife habitat and commercial use.
OTHER FACTS
1.   There is no conclusive scientific evidence that the northern spotted owl population is either increasing or decreasing; no reliable information on their reproductive rates in young forests; and no scientific definition of "biologically effective" owl habitat.
2.   Until recently, no effort has been made to count northern spotted owls in wilderness areas or other set asides, or on private land. More owls are being found as the search expands.
3.   Nesting northern spotted owl pairs have been found in remnant old growth stands left after harvest, which is evidence that managed forest settings can provide suitable habitat.
4.   More than 200 individual northern spotted owls and 20 breeding pairs have been found in the past 3 months in northern California in a mixed-age, managed forest. More are being found in second growth timber, which raises serious scientific questions about the owl's dependence on old growth forests.
FOR MORE INFORMATION:
A RESOURCE BOOKLET IS AVAILABLE:
Contact:
Northwest Forest Resources Council --- 222-9505 1500 S.W. First Ave. Suite 770 Portland. OR 97210.
The owl, the people, and the science were constantly being buffeted back and forth. At about the same time that Rep. VanLeeuwen attempted to get some reality into the spotted owl argument, an analysis of the situation came from a new point of view—an attorney's. A partner in a major Portland law firm reviewed the owl situation and found flaws in the arguments supporting the contention that the spotted owl was going extinct. His review catches the critical elements in the argument as it stood in the summer of 1989.

"Although numerous articles have appeared in the press, including *Oregon Business,* concerning the claims that the northern spotted owl is an endangered or threatened species, few if any, have addressed the scientific basis for such claims. Until a few years ago little was known about the spotted owl because it is a nocturnal bird, and few people had ever seen one.

"Over one-half of all the timberland in Oregon is owned by the federal government. From that federal land, Congress has created over 3 million acres of national park, wilderness, scenic, and other specially protected areas in Oregon. Within those specially protected areas logging is not permitted.

"The current controversy over the spotted owl really goes back to the issue of how much federal forestland should be set aside as wilderness areas. The Oregon Forest Wilderness Act of 1984, which doubled the size of wilderness areas in Oregon to over 2 million acres and which specifically addressed how much low elevation timber should be preserved, was based on a compromise worked out by the Oregon congressional delegation who thought it had been accepted by both the environmentalists and the timber industry. Under that law, the national forestlands not included in wilderness areas were released by Congress for multiple-use management, including logging. However, almost as soon as the wilderness bill was signed into law, the Oregon Natural Resources Council and some other environmental groups set out to prevent logging in areas of old growth timber which had been released by Congress.

"Since 1937, Congress has recognized that the nonspecially protected federal timberlands in Oregon should be managed on a 'sustained yield' basis to provide a permanent source of timber in order to contribute 'to the economic stability of local communities and industries.' For over 50 years the federal government has been managing its commercial timberlands on a long-term basis so that no more timber is cut each year than is grown annually.

"In recent decades, timber from federal lands has become the sole source of logs for many of Oregon's mills because the timber from private lands was logged first. Even though many of those lands were reforested, the second growth on most private lands will not be large enough to harvest for several more decades,

"Because Congress has chosen not to give old growth any special protection outside of specially protected areas, the environmentalists have chosen to use the spotted owl as a 'surrogate' to stop the logging old growth timberlands. In fact, as Richard Stahl of the Sierra Club Legal Defense Fund, has stated, "Thank goodness the spotted owl evolved in the Northwest, for if it hadn't, we'd have to genetically engineer it."

"Although Stahl did not engineer the spotted owl, Stahl and Russell Lande, an associate professor at the University of Chicago, together have largely engineered the current controversy over whether or not the spotted owl is threatened with extinction.

"The Sierra Club Legal Defense Fund has provided attorneys to represent the Audubon Society and the other plaintiffs in all of the major lawsuits involving the spotted owl. Lande is the Sierra Club's primary expert witness in those lawsuits to support the claim that the spotted owl is an endangered species. In 1984 Stahl sought out Lande to write a report concerning the survival of the spotted owl, although Lande had never written a paper before concerning the possible extinction of any species. At that time Stahl was employed by the National Wildlife Federation. With information furnished from Stahl, Lande prepared a report in 1985 using a mathematical model that he developed to predict the owl's likely extinction.

"A Behavior Model

"That model contains a number of assumptions concerning the spotted owl's behavior and its habitat, including that the spotted owl can only survive where there are large areas of old growth forests. Although each pair of spotted owls actually uses a core area of approximately 300 acres, based on Lande's testimony the environmentalists are seeking an injunction covering a 2.1-mile radius of land for each owl site. A circle of that radius contains approximately 9,000 acres, or 30 times the core area required by a pair of owls.

"To put that into perspective, one acre is approximately the size of a football field. There are 400 owl sites on Bureau of Land Management forest lands and at least twice that number on U.S. Forest Service (USFS) lands.

"Lande in his 1985 report, concludes that the owl's population is decreasing at '... a rate of about 8% per year. In 26 years it will be reduced to about 10% of its current size, and ... it is expected to become extinct within roughly ... 97 years.'

"Normally papers which are published in scientific journals are first submitted to a group of the author's peers for review before an article is printed. Lande's report was given to Stahl for review, but it was never submitted to any scientific journal for publication. Instead, Lande recently testified in a lawsuit that it was written to 'be distributed by the National Wildlife Federation from the Portland office to anybody who requested it.'

"It was actually submitted by the environmentalists to the U.S. Fish & Wildlife Service, the USFS, the BLM, and other agencies to support their claim that it was "new scientific evidence" that the spotted owl was an endangered species and that it was necessary to stop the logging of old growth in order to protect it. It also has been used as a basis for lawsuits brought by the environmentalists against those federal agencies claiming that the spotted owl needs to be protected.

"Although not published in any scientific journal, Lande's report did not escape peer review. When Lande recently testified, he named eight other individuals who, in his opinion, were qualified to analyze data in the field of population viability analysis. Two that Lande named were Professors Dan Goodman and Mark Boyce. Goodman, who is a professor at Montana State University, was requested by the Fish & Wildlife Service to review both Lande's report and another analysis model done by the USFS.

"Concerning his review of the Lande and Forest Service models, Goodman stated, 'I concur with [Dr. Mark] Shaffer [of the Fish & Wildlife Service] in his principal substantive criticism of the two viability analyses.' Goodman went on to state: 'I believe the criticism Shaffer raises, and the other I raise, are sufficiently severe that neither of the two viability analyses can be taken seriously.'

"He further stated, 'The fatal criticism, in my view, encompasses both the analytical methods and the empirical database of the two viability analyses, both of which are inexcusably inadequate in both regards.' Goodman also characterizes Lande's 'theoretical model' as 'clever, but not necessarily realistic.'

"Boyce, professor of zoology and physiology at the University of Wyoming, was equally critical of Lande's model, stating that it did not have sufficient statistical reliability to justify its use as a basis for major forest management decisions regarding the spotted owl.

"However, the most stinging criticism of Lande's model came from a source that was the least expected, the National Audubon Society. In 1986 the society published a conservation report from a Blue Ribbon Panel of experts it has appointed to study the spotted owl.

"The panel took Lande's conclusion that the spotted owl population was declining at the rate of 8% per year and then projected the owl's population backward for a period of 20 years (four generations). Using Lande's model there should have been 38 million pairs of owls in the Pacific Northwest, which the Blue Ribbon Panel termed 'an absurdity.'

"Apparently stung by these criticisms, Lande redid his analysis using new data. In August 1987 he submitted his new paper for publication in a scientific journal that is published in West Germany. In his second paper Lande came to the conclusion that his model showed that from a statistical standpoint the population of the spotted owl was '...not significantly different from that for a stable population, supporting the contention that the population currently may be near a demographic equilibrium.'

"After Lande's new paper was submitted for publication, the attorneys for the Sierra Legal Defense Fund and the environmental law clinic at the University of Oregon Law School brought an action on behalf of a number of environmentalist groups seeking an injunction preventing all BLM old growth timber sales involving potential spotted owl sites in Oregon.

"In October 1987 those same attorneys submitted to the court an affidavit signed by Lande in which he again claimed that the spotted owl was declining at the rate of 8% per year and would likely become extinct within approximately 100 years, even though he had already written his new report stating that the spotted owl population was statistically stable.

"After the U.S. District Court dismissed the BLM case in April 1988 the same attorneys appealed to the U.S. Court of Appeals and sought an emergency injunction based in part on Lande's affidavit and again not mentioning that Lande had submitted a new report for publication which contradicted his affidavit,

"In August 1988 Lande's new paper was finally published. Recently while under cross examination by Mark Rutzick, counsel for the Northwest Forest Resource Council, Lande admitted that at the time he signed his 1987 affidavit he did not think that it was 'most likely' that the spotted owl would become extinct in roughly 100 years as he had stated. He went on to state, 'I wasn't sure of the exact rate of decline or the time of extinction.'

"Second Paper Criticized

"When Lande's second paper was published, it did not fare much better in the eyes of his peers. The pre-publication reviews of that article criticized the meagerness of his database, his assumptions, and his attempt to make specific management recommendations from a general model.

"As one critic stated: '"The database on the spotted owl is pretty thin. This is not just a theory paper, but one that attempts to make specific recommendations. Doing this with such a speculative database seems very risky.' Another critic urged caution about the 'political ramifications' of the paper. .

"Lande's basic thesis in his second paper is still that spotted owls can only survive in old growth habitat; therefore, it is necessary to stop logging all old growth at this time. By Lande's estimate, 38% of the old growth on national forest lands remains uncut and that in order to protect the spotted owl from extinction, it is necessary to protect of least 21 % of old growth on national forest lands.

"However, Lande has admitted he did not include in either his 1985 or his 1988 model the old growth forests in national parks, wildernesses, and other specially protected areas, the total acreage of which exceeds the amount of old growth necessary to protect the spotted owl using his model. Finally, Lande has admitted that even though he has written two papers concerning what habitat is necessary for the spotted owl, he has never seen one! They are difficult to find in Chicago.

"Unfortunately, the Fish & Wildlife Service's recent finding that the spotted owl should be considered for 'threatened' species status continues to cite Lande's reports in support of its decision on that basis that 'Lande's analysis demonstrates a plausible risk of extinction... " An analysis that is merely 'plausible' would seem to he a very thin rope by which to hang Oregon's major industry over a chasm of economic chaos, and let it twist for a year or two, while the Fish & Wildlife Service makes a decision concerning the owl's future status.

"The ultimate fate of the spotted owl probably depends less on the actions of man than it does on those of other owls. The great homed owl is the natural predator of the spotted owl and especially enjoys feeding on juvenile spotted owls. As the Audubon Society Blue Ribbon Panel report points out, the barred owl, which is closely related to the spotted owl, is now moving into the forests of the Pacific Northwest. Because the barred owl is more aggressive, it is likely to displace the spotted owl in areas of habitat which they share. As this competition plays out, it is the owls, and not man, that will eventually determine the survival of the fittest.

"A $16 Million Loss

"According to affidavits filed with the courts by Governor Neil Goldschmidt and others, the injunction by the Court of Appeals cost the taxpayers of the state of Oregon over $16 million in lost timber revenues, and the current injunctions could cost several times that much this year. This does not include the impacts to the economy caused by mill closures and the resulting unemployment of' mill workers. In seeking to protect the spotted owl, the environmentalists have consistently argued through their attorneys that the human, social, and economic consequences that the citizens of Oregon would suffer if the logging of old growth is halted are irrelevant.

"Many of the environmental groups are national organizations with no long-term stake in Oregon's future, but are waging a well-funded campaign to stop the logging of old growth here. They include the San Francisco-based Sierra Club, the New York-based Natural Resources Defense Council and National Audubon Society, and the Washington, DC Wilderness Society and National Wildlife Federation.

"The current annual budgets of these organizations are approximately: National Wildlife Federation, $64 million; National Audubon Society, $29 million, The Sierra Club, $26 million, The Natural Resources Defense Council, $12 million; and the Wilderness Society $ 10 million. Together their annual budgets exceed the state's annual expenditures for natural resources by more than $6O million.

"Even the Oregon Natural Resources Defense Council has an annual budget of approximately $500,000, and it obtains free legal services at the taxpayers' expense by being represented in lawsuits, such as the BLM spotted owl case, by the environmental law clinic at the University of Oregon Law School....

"The National Audubon Society Blue Ribbon Panel's report recommended man- aging forests for minimum of 1,500 pair of spotted owls in the Pacific Northwest in order to provide for the survival of the species. This would actually allow for a 25% decline over the confirmed level of 2500 pairs known to exist as of the time the panel's report was published in 1986.

"More recent studies show that there are about 2,500 pairs of spotted owls in the Pacific Northwest. Because spotted owls are constantly being discovered in new locations, including in second growth stands, it appears that there is little likelihood of the population declining to the minimum level recommended by the Blue Ribbon Panel during the foreseeable future.

"A biologist for the National Audubon Society, who has actually seen spotted owls, recently testified that spotted owl habitat includes both old growth and '"mature' trees (100 to 200 years old), Mature timber is the age of rotation managed by Oregon forest planners to provide lumber for future generations in perpetuity. After a tree reaches maturity, its growth rate slows down, and by the time it becomes 'old growth,' the wood often begins to rot.

"The ramifications of the Audubon biologist's testimony are two-fold. If spotted owls will live in mature timber, then Lande is wrong concerning his assertion that the owls require an old growth habitat. This also means that there is a lot more habitat available to the spotted owl than the remaining old growth. On the other hand if the spotted owl is truly threatened with extinction and will also live in mature second growth timber, loggers in Oregon may be restricted to cutting Christmas trees.

"Earth First!, one of the most radical environmental organizations, is already agitating to restrict private landowners from logging their second growth timber. Dave Foreman, a founder of Earth First!, was quoted in a recent interview that his goal was 'to reduce [the] human population to about 100 million worldwide, destroy the industrial infrastructure, and see wilderness with its full complement of species restored throughout the world.'

"Oregonians should keep in mind that Earth First!'s agenda today is usually the Oregon Natural Resources Council's and Sierra Club's agendas for tomorrow. The environmentalists have already brought at least one lawsuit to stop logging in second growth timber in order to protect a pair of owls. If the Sierra Club eventually finds a spotted owl on a Christmas tree farm, Santa Claus, along with the Oregon logger, may become an endangered species."[203]

Chadsey's extended explanation captured the essence of the spotted owl issue for Oregon in the late 1980s. Nevertheless, the search for more lasting solutions to the owl problem continued. Senator Packwood sought new rules for the appeals process for federal timber sales.[204] Environmentalists reported they were reserving judgment. Timber sales could be challenged in court only after all administrative appeals had been exhausted. Meanwhile, it appeared that the U. S. Senate would not get around to considering the Hatfield-Adams amendment to the Appropriations Bill before the summer recess of the Senate.[205]

In the timber dependent communities people were hurting. A human-interest story[206] told how FISH, an agency that provides food, lodging, gas and transportation to the needy, was running out of funds. It was reported that the needs in Lebanon had increased recently. "A lot of people are out of work because of mill closures and some welfare programs have been cut."

The chief of the Forest Service, Dale Robertson, spoke publicly and said that the proposed rules for protecting the spotted owl in Washington, Oregon and California were too restrictive. The rules would make it impossible for the agency to get out the timber cut called for in Congressional directives.[207]

Earth First! kept the pressure on all logging activity. They were protesting a timber sale on the Siuslaw National Forest that had been awarded, after due consideration of all applicable laws, to a timber company. Nevertheless, the sale was being protested because it was near a wilderness area.[208]

Despite the dire predictions of what federal timber might be available for harvesting and processing, the timber industry continued to contribute to the political process. The timber industry was reported to have contributed about 1/3 of a million dollars to the campaign chests of federal and state lawmakers.[209]

Plans were still being made for future timber harvests on the national forests despite court orders halting approved sales. On the Sweet Home Ranger District, Willamette National Forest, nearly two thirds of the sales were enjoined. Nevertheless, plans for future sales were being made.[210]

The *Yellow Ribbon Express,* the newsletter of the Communities for a Greater Oregon, implored its readers to write to congressmen and urge multiple-use of the national forests. It also urged readers to contact Paul Newman, the Stroh Brewing Company and Turner Broadcasting Company regarding the mis-information in the up-coming broadcast on forestry in the Northwest on TBS.[211] Pre-broadcast publicity indicated that "unless logging is stopped the last of our virgin timber lands will be turned into little more than commercial tree plantations."

Obviously, the supporters of the broadcast did not recognize or accept the facts about existing reserved areas that Rep. VanLeeuwen listed in her information sheet cited above.

The U. S. Fish and Wildlife Service (USFWS) was starting hearings on the listing of the owl. There was much confusion about what the agency planned to do to protect the owl.[212]

Rep. VanLeeuwen, after reading that the President had discussed environmental issues with Robert Redford, wrote the President and asked for equal time. She also sent him supporting documents and pointed out to him the dire straits of timber dependent communities in her district.[213] Rep. VanLeeuwen also made contact with Stroh Brewing Company and wrote to one the company's public relations officers concerning the up-coming broadcast on northwestern forestry. She cited the article reproduced above by Mr. Chadsey.[214] Senator Hatfield was asked for help in getting the National Humane Society to correct misinformation on the amount of old growth reported in a recent publication of the Society.[215]

The USFWS is charged with protecting endangered species, no matter what, under the Endangered Species Act. The U. S. Forest Service (USFS) is charged with managing the national forests under a complex set of laws, such as the National Forest Management Act. As the spotted owl hearings were begun by the USFWS the testimony of the Deputy Director of Wildlife and Fisheries, USFS, captures the essence of the conflict in laws and information regarding the forests and the owls. On August 14, 1989 Hal Salwasser testified before a USFWS hearing in Portland, OR:

"The Forest Service manages 70 percent of the currently identified habitat for the northern spotted owl, more than 4.8 million acres. Over half, more than 2.6 million of these acres, are not subject to timber harvest. They include 913,000 acres in wilderness and other reserved lands, 983,000 acres not suited for timber management, and 668,000 acres in designated spotted owl habitat areas in lands that would otherwise be suited for timber production.

"The Forest Service has carried out or funded over 80 percent of the research, inventories, surveys, and studies ever conducted on the spotted owl. These efforts began in the early 1970s, and have increased yearly. They currently involve over 200 biologists, hundreds of other Forest Service personnel and volunteers, and over $5 million per year.

"The northern spotted owl has been classified as a sensitive species by the Forest Service in California, Oregon, and Washington for more than 10 years. Habitats of sensitive species in the national forests are managed to maintain viable populations, with numbers and distributions that preclude the need to list those species as threatened or endangered.

"Beginning in the mid-1970's, the Forest Service has protected habitats for spotted owls while managing National Forests for many other uses and values required by law. In 1976, Congress strengthened the Forest Service's mandate for stewardship of the National Forests by   including the goal to provide for diversity of plant and animal communities as part of overall multiple-use objectives.   With the help of a committee of scientists, the Forest Service interpreted the goal to mean, in part, that National Forests should be managed to maintain viable populations of all native and desired normative vertebrates.   In 1982, the Forest Service strengthened the requirement by defining a viable population as one which has numbers and distributions that will ensure continued existence of the species, well-distributed throughout its range on National Forests.

"The goal of maintaining diversity while meeting overall multiple use objectives produces the national forest planning issue for spotted owls. And it is a different issue than the one the Fish & Wildlife Service must now address in considering listing the spotted owl as threatened. Both agencies are charged with perpetuating native species of wildlife through conservation of the ecosystems which give them life. The listing consideration stops there.

"National Forest planning goes further. Because the spotted owl represents many other plant and animal species associated with mature and old forests, and because its habitats are also prime sources of timber supplies, the forest planning issue is more complex than the listing issue: what is the best way to perpetuate spotted owl populations and other plants and animals of old-growth ecosystems while sustaining the production of timber and other resources people need from their national forests. The listing question must be addressed solely on biological merits. But such a narrow consideration begs the question of a prudent balance between perpetuation of native wildlife and sustainable uses of forest resources that are vital to our nation's economy and to people's livelihoods. This is the fundamental public policy issue that the spotted owl brings before the American people.

"In August 1988, the Pacific Northwest Region of the Forest Service completed a Supplement to the Environmental Impact Statement for an amendment to the Regional Guide for spotted owl habitat planning. Based on that environmental statement, the Chief of the Forest Service decided, in December 1988, to increase habitat protection measures in the national forests of Oregon and Washington with the intent to assure long-term population viability for the northern spotted owl.

"In his decision, the Chief of the Forest Service reduced the life of current planning guidelines' for owl habitat in the Pacific Northwest Region from 10 to 5 years. He endorsed stronger interagency coordination and intensified the continuing, cooperative program of inventories, research, and monitoring of spotted owls and their habitats. He expanded the size of spotted owl habitat areas protected in the network of suitable owl habitats distributed throughout the national forests of Oregon and Washington. He committed the Forest Service to strengthen habitat protection at any time new information showed that necessary for long-term viability. And he directed that habitats in Oregon and Washington be connected with a similar habitat network for owls in the national forests in California.

"Northern spotted owls prefer old-growth conifer and mixed-conifer forests, or mature stands with old-growth elements as their habitats. There are an estimated 6.9 million acres of such habitat in the entire range of the northern spotted owl--about 40 percent of the 17.5 million acres believed to have been present in the mid-1800s. The current habitat is estimated to be capable of supporting about 2,400 breeding pairs. The 4.8 million acres of habitat in the national forests are estimated to be capable of supporting 1,790 breeding pairs, 75 percent of the estimated total population. Exact population numbers are not possible due to the difficulty of complete annual censuses of the species.

"The Environmental Impact Statement developed by the Forest Service for forest planning direction in Oregon and Washington indicated that habitat conditions sufficient to support a total population of over 2,000 breeding pairs, well distributed over the geographic range of the species, yet each within close enough proximity to insure genetic and demographic interchange, would provide a high likelihood of long-term continued existence for spotted owls. It also showed that special protection was immediately needed to insure continued existence, especially measures to minimize habitat fragmentation and possible isolation of small subpopulations. Unknowns and uncertainty were such that intense research and monitoring were essential to verify assumptions made in planning for population viability and to adjust habitat protection as needed.

"The Forest Service (with substantial help from the Congress), environmental groups, state wildlife agencies, volunteers, and the timber industry have intensified owl inventories and surveys since the environmental statement was filed. Much of this has occurred since information was provided to the Fish & Wildlife Service for its status review concerning spotted owls in February 1989. These new data will be used to test the validity of assumptions and methods used in the current viability analysis. Research studies and monitoring now underway will eventually lead to new evaluations and revisions of protection measures as needed for population viability. Preliminary results of these studies will be submitted to the Fish and Wildlife Service for consideration in its listing decision.

"Long-term trends in habitats and populations of spotted owls will depend on current and many future decisions. For the next 5 years, the Forest Service has implemented regulatory mechanisms to secure 668,000 acres of northern spotted owl habitat on lands that would otherwise have been planned for timber harvest. These acres occur in over 600 designated areas to ensure that no habitat for breeding pairs is farther than 6 miles from at least one, often 2 or 3, other such habitats.

"Annual timber sales are being reduced by about 300 million board feet in Oregon, Washington, and California to reflect the owl habitat removed from forested lands allocated to timber harvest. During the next 5 years, about 230,000 acres of northern spotted owl habitat would be logged to provide timber while inventories, monitoring, and research on spotted owls continue. This logging is estimated to reduce habitat capability for spotted owls by about 5 percent of the current population of northern spotted owls in the national forests.

"In 1994, more than 1. 9 million acres of northern spotted owl habitat on national forest lands suited for timber harvest will remain to be considered in revising habitat protection. These acres will be available to augment the owl habitat network if new information shows that necessary. The Forest Service calls this approach to spotted owl habitat protection adaptive management.

"The adaptive management approach is not ideal for spotted owls; saving all remaining habitat is ideal for owls. Nor is it ideal for timber supplies; 668,000 acres are removed from lands where timber might have been harvested. However, it does protect 95 percent of the habitat capability for spotted owls during the next 5 years, and it provides for 95 percent of the timber harvests that would have been available without added protection of spotted owl habitat. Is current habitat protection satisfactory for long-term viability? We don't know yet. That is why the Forest Service is preceding for only 5 years and spending more than $5 million per year on spotted owl inventories, research, monitoring, and evaluations. When new information shows that adjustments in habitat protection are needed, they will be made.

"The northern spotted owl is a sensitive species. It needs--and is receiving--special protection. The northern spotted owl, its habitat, and associated wildlife species are significant ecological resources. The Forest Service has full responsibility for perpetuating all native wildlife in the national forests. We have implemented policies and regulatory mechanisms with the aim to assure long-term survival of the northern spotted owl on those forests. These mechanisms include habitat protection, interagency coordination, research and monitoring, and a commitment to adjust habitat protection as new information shows that necessary. With protection under these measures, the future of the northern spotted owl in the national forests will be secure without protection under the Endangered Species Act.

"In the other public hearing, Forest Service officials will describe how the forest planning and decision-making process is used to ensure that owls are protected while carrying out timber management activities; how research and development efforts contribute to the adaptive management approach, and what the current program of habitat protection looks like on a national forest. "[216]

Salwasser's statement was a clear description of the condition of the owl and the way the national forests were being managed. As we shall see, the USFWS did not consider the efforts of the USFS to be sufficient for the protection of the northern spotted owl.

Those interested in the viability of the timber industry, and the communities dependent on a viable industry, were not sure the efforts of the USFS would be sufficient to convince the USFWS. The timber industry announced a national public relations campaign to counter the efforts of environmentalists and the media to close down harvest of national forest timber.[217] The same issue of the *Democrat Herald* carried another article about the efforts of activists to stop all timber harvest in several national forests in the Pacific Northwest.[218]

Rep. VanLeeuwen sent out an advisory memorandum to her constituents urging them to write the USFWS before September 21, 1989, telling them why the northern spotted owl should not be listed.[219] She suggested to her audience that they should mention that there was no good scientific evidence supporting the listing of the owl, that owls had not been counted in wilderness areas, and that nesting pairs had been found in managed forests.

The newspaper reports of the USFWS August 14, 1989 hearing were varied. For example, the Eugene *Register Guard* reported that 75 people had testified at the Portland hearing. The majority of the article quoted those who wanted timber harvest stopped. However, the story was published under a picture of a logger holding his small son. The story quoted him as saying he was scared. The testimony of Dr. Salwasser, quoted above, was covered by a single sentence paragraph: "Official representatives of the U. S. Forest Service and U. S. Bureau of Land Management testified Monday that the owl does not need to be listed under the Endangered Species Act because current forest management practices already assure the bird's survival." Another paragraph cast another light on that testimony: "Unofficial representatives of the Forest Service said they support the listing of the owl, acknowledging that the bird's habits and habitat needs still are not fully understood."[220]

The hearing in Portland was followed by one in Redding, CA. There a large turnout of people supporting the timber industry, estimated at 3500, heard biologists for the timber industry report that there were many more owls than the USFWS was considering. A USFWS biologist was quoted as saying that a decision on listing was several months away. He also discounted the importance of numbers of owls.[221]

All sorts of attempts were made to assure people that the forests of Oregon were being managed wisely. *TIMBER!*, a publication of Timber Resource Education, Inc., devoted an issue to the BLM and its forest management efforts. It headlined the story "BLM Lands: Model of Sustained Yield."[222]

Meanwhile, programs were being strengthened that would support people who for one reason or another needed help finding employment, for example, laid off timber workers.[223]

And, although the final decision on listing of the owl was yet to be made, the potential listing was having an influence on timber sales from federal land. For example, BLM was going through a series of reviews of planned timber sales with USFWS in the Coos Bay District. Of 23 million board feet planned for auction in September, all but 6.4 million board feet had been pulled. For the fiscal year ending at the end of September 1989,

254 million board feet had been planned for sale; due to concern for the owl it was estimated that at most 163 million board feet would be sold.[224]

How and who should manage forests was a continuing debate. Some thought that if forests were privately owned they should be managed as the owner wished under the restrictions of the Oregon Forest Practices Act. Some thought that federal land should be managed under the existing federal statutes. Others felt differently. As the debate raged over the owl, a group called Cascade Holistic Economic Consultants, of Eugene, OR, held a conference on reform of the USFS.

A speaker at the conference was Jerry Franklin, a professor at the University of Washington and an employee of the research arm of the USFS. He urged the protection of all forests, not just old growth, as a way to protect "all elements of biological diversity." Many speakers at the conference attended by some 150 people agreed with Franklin and sought ways to change the USFS.[225]

The last of four hearings the USFWS held on the spotted owl was in Eugene, OR. The impact of the hearings on the decision process was minimal. Barry Mulder, coordinator of the service's spotted owl listing process, was reported as saying, "[The hearings were] pretty much what we expected. In terms of new, significant information, we haven't heard anything new or different. This Forum isn't set up to get a lot of new, scientific information. It's mainly a public forum."[226] Reading the news accounts one gets a sense of the Service giving people on both sides of the argument an opportunity to vent their frustrations; the agency has made up its mind and is not about to change.

As August came to a close, supporters of the forest industry continued their efforts to stave off the listing of the northern spotted owl. A truck loaded with wood products was sent off to Washington, D. C. to be used as a rallying point for the workers in the woods;[227] Senator Packwood was still trying to get the Hatfield-Adams amendments passed,[228] and Rep. VanLeeuwen wrote to a House committee chairman in Washington, D. C. pleading for understanding of the plight of her constituents if the national forests were shut down to timber harvest.[229] As we shall see, all these efforts were for naught.

CHAPTER ELEVEN

SEPTEMBER 1989

Hope springs eternal in the human breast, according to an old saying. Events in this month bear that out. "Oregon timber delegation heading to Washington" was a story about a grass-roots effort to get Congress to pass the Hatfield-Adams amendment.[230] Rep. VanLeeuwen was a member of the group. She reported that the purpose of the trip was to lobby for the passage of the Hatfield-Adams amendment. Members of the delegation expected to spend a week in Washington. "We hope to get them to look at the real facts. We've got to put it in a perspective they understand," she said.

The 9th Circuit Court of Appeals lifted its ban on sales of old growth timber by the BLM.[231] The court said the federal law carried by Senator Hatfield in 1987 and 1988 precluded the environmental challenge. That law said an existing BLM timber management plan could not be challenged on the basis of new information. The BLM's decision to make an "intentional trade-off of owls for economic gain" is protected from environmental lawsuits by the Hatfield measure, said Chief Judge Alfred Goodwin in the 3-0 decision.

The "fine print" of the decision, however, showed the timber industry's victory to be limited. A follow-up story reported that only 66 million board feet would be immediately available for sale. An industry spokesman expressed the fear that with such small volumes the competition would cause timber bids to skyrocket. The spokesman got in a plug for the Hatfield-Adams amendment, saying it was the real solution to the problem of managing timber from the federal forests administered by the U S Forest Service and BLM.[232]

Union members rallied for the Hatfield-Adams amendment.[233] Environmentalists wrote Op-Ed pieces arguing for the preservation of old growth.[234] Loggers began to break ranks in some places. One report noted that less than 1000 workers showed up at a rally in Salem, even though companies had given them time off and provided transportation to the rally.[235] In other ways the grass roots activity was intense. Two loaded log trucks and 150 people made the long trip to Washington to lobby for the Hatfield-Adams amendment.[236]

Rhetoric surrounding the lobbying for and against the amendment generated some heated words. Andy Kerr, Oregon Natural Resources Council, was quoted as saying, "The Hatfield-Adams rider will kill spotted owls as sure as a drunken logger with a shotgun."[237] The drunken logger statement stirred one retired logger to write the editor. He said, in part:

"As a retired logger of some 40 years, I deeply resent his (Kerr's) not-so-subtle attempt at character and professional assassination. I realize that for many years loggers were represented as indigent ne'er-do-wells with a penchant for drinking and rowdiness in general. Perhaps this was a somewhat valid characterization then, but believe me, Mr. Kerr, in spite of your continued misconception, times have changed.

"Loggers and their families are responsible taxpayers who own their own homes, participate in community affairs and are subject to all the joys, hardships and tribulations that affect everyone else.

"You would stigmatize loggers with a fault or indiscretion that supposedly sets them apart from the rest of society. I would state, just as adamantly, that a drunken lawyer, doctor or yes, even an environmentalist, could do equally as much damage.

"You have only to look at the environmentalists who, in their sobriety and with deliberate intent, created a scenario for disaster for many of the citizens of the Northwest.

"I seriously doubt that 10,000 "drunken loggers" could do the damage that these troublemakers, masquerading under the guise of "saviors," are contemplating. I can only hope that his insensitive and disparaging remark will awaken people to the disdain with which the elitists of the environmentalists' ranks regard the working man and his welfare."

William C. Medlock, Sweet Home.[238]

The Hatfield-Adams amendment to the Interior Department's appropriation bill continued to generate intense debate, and the intensity was increasing.[239] Behind the scenes other congressmen were attempting to modify the amendment to make it more acceptable to environmentalists. Key lawmakers in this effort were Rep. Sidney Yates, Chairman of the subcommittee, Rep. Les AuCoin, Oregon, and Rep. Norm Dicks, Washington.[240] These representatives, along with Hatfield and Adams, were attempting to craft a compromise that could be passed by Congress. What they were offering was a reduction in the amount of timber to be sold, more court access and review, and more protection for spotted owl sites. The compromise faced tough sledding as the month came to a close. Rep. Yates was withholding endorsement.[241] Further efforts were made to work out a solution.[242] There was little hope that the legislation would be enacted.[243]

While the maneuvering continued in Congress, other facets of the debate about forest resources and their use continued. A spokesman for a timber group posted a positive story about timber supply and the health of the industry—if logs were available.[244] With reduced timber harvest on federal land there would be less money available for maintenance of recreational facilities—campgrounds, trails—than previously. The solution? Charge for hunting, fishing, hiking and camping.[245] This seemed a reasonable solution. Earlier in the month a story reported that a study conducted by Oregon State University researchers had found that restrictions on use of wildernesses would be acceptable by the users.[246] Surely a fee system would add to the restriction and make the wilderness experience more meaningful.

Earlier in the year we learned that many thought the treatment of the old-growth question by the Turner Broadcasting System was too biased. Supporters of the timber industry had protested to Stroh Brewery, a sponsor for the program by TBS, and the brewer had withdrawn support. Nevertheless, the network was standing by the show. It was attempting to find other companies to support the program.[247]

The grass-roots activists were going through a period of trial and reorganization. The Oregon Project, a yellow ribbon coalition supporting multiple use of federal land had lost its identity according an article in the Lebanon *Express*. The article went on to say that Communities for a Greater Oregon (CGO) seemed to be an organization with which the Project could work. Attempts were being made to make CGO a more representative force in the spotted owl/natural resource battle.[248]

The number of northern spotted owls that occupy the forests of the Pacific Northwest had never been one on which all parties could agree. As we saw earlier, the actual number was not important to some people; the owl was being used as a surrogate to stop timber harvest. However, the number of owls was controversial. Considerable evidence showed that there were more owls than the USFWS assumed and that the species was not in decline.[249] The lead paragraphs in the article, a copy from *Evergreen* Magazine, said:

"There is no conclusive evidence that spotted owl populations are decreasing.

"Although the scientific community has learned a great deal about the tiny owl over the last year, there is still much to be learned about its habitat requirement.

"What is now known can be summed up in three statements:

"First, there are many more spotted owls than was once thought.

"Second, while spotted owls may prefer old growth nesting sites, the birds definitely range over a diversity of forest habitats, presumably in their daily search for food, principally small rodents.

"Third, with increasing frequency, spotted owls are being found in second growth forests, including private timberlands replanted over the last 30 to 40 years.[20]

The article goes on to make the argument that the spotted owl controversy isn't about spotted owls but is being used to expand wilderness areas in federal forests. President Bill Clinton designated an additional 60 million acres or so of federal forest as forever roadless just before leaving office at the beginning of 2002.

It was during this month that the issue of more control of private forest operations, that is, controls beyond the Forest Practices Act that was presently on the books. A case in point: A privately owned tract of timber in the North Santiam River watershed in Oregon. Environmentalists were seeking to convince the Los Angeles based Times Mirror Company to forego harvesting its land near the Opal Creek watershed in the North Santiam Basin.[250]

Earlier, on another front, the Oregon Natural Resources Council had won an appeal of a timber sale on the Winema National Forest, located west of Klamath Lake in southern Oregon, on the basis of the failure of that Forest to consider the impact of the logging on the bald eagle population.[251]

The effort to stop logging, at least on federal land, got up close and personal. Extreme measures were recommended. Earth First! may have taken the most extreme position up to that time. In the organization's journal this suggestion was made:

"Are you terminally ill with a wasting disease? Do you have AIDS, ALS, brain cancer, or syphilis? Don't go out with a whimper; go out with a bang! Undertake an eco-kamikaze mission.

"Yes, terminally ill Earth defenders can perform the ultimate act of Ecodefence while cheating the Grim reaper of all the wasting and suffering that precedes these hideous, industrial age deaths.

"Seek martyrdom at Glen Canyon Dam. Blow up yourself and that monstrosity. Free the Wild Colorado.

"The possibilities for terminally ill warriors are limitless. Dams from the Columbia and the Colorado to the Connecticut are crying to be blown to smithereens, as are the industrial polluters, the headquarters of oil spilling corporations, fur warehouses, paper mills…No doubt you already have a favorite target in your own watershed."[252]

From the displaced loggers to the opponents of logging, the feelings ran deep as fall 1989 came to the Pacific Northwest.

CHAPTER TWELVE

FALL 1989

Congress finally passed the Hatfield-Adams Amendment in October 1989. It called for the sale of 7.7 million board feet by October 1, 1990.[253] The amendment had been hotly debated since the Timber Summit in June 1989 in Salem.

Passage of the amendment touched off a flurry of activity. Immediately protests and legal action by environmentalists occupied the courts. Both BLM and the Forest Service were being hit by lawsuits.[254] The position being taken by environmental groups was spelled out in an Associated Press story from Seattle. The first parts of the story detailed the issues from the environmentalists' point of view:

"Environmentalists have challenged a legislative "truce" on management of Northwest old-growth forests and told a federal court their lawsuit to protect the northern spotted owl should proceed.

"Vic Sher, lawyer for the Sierra Club Legal Defense Fund, said Thursday that environmentalist plaintiffs in the lawsuit believe Congress acted unconstitutionally in crafting the one-year compromise designed to meet both the needs of the timber industry and the threatened owl.

"The pact was reached after lengthy negotiations among members of Congress and tacked onto an Interior appropriations measure that was signed Monday by President Bush.

"The legislation will allow the Forest Service and the Bureau of Land Management to sell old-growth timber in the Northwest over the next 12 months but requires the agencies to start protecting the old-growth stands that provide prime habitat for the spotted owl.

"Sher said the Sierra Fund disagreed with a section in which Congress in effect took away from the courts the authority to hear environmentalist challenges to the Forest Service's management of national forests.

"'The problem that it poses is that Congress (under Article 3 of the Constitution) cannot tell a court how to apply existing law to a pending case. That is something only courts can,' said Sher.

"'Conservationists can't condone wreaking havoc on the Constitution any more than we can condone wreaking havoc on the public's forests,' said James Monteith, executive director of the Oregon Natural Resources Council.

"Sher said that after Bush signed the legislation Monday, U. S. District Judge William Dwyer of Seattle asked all parties to the lawsuit to file opinions on what the next step should be." [255]

In the period between the congressional action on Oct. 7 and the signing of the legislation by the President on Oct. 23, other aspects of the old-growth owl debate were examined. Larry Irwin, a researcher for the forest industry's environmental research organization, The National Council of the Paper Industry for Air and Stream Improvement (NCASI), reported to the Albany (OR) Chamber of Commerce that spotted owls were living and reproducing in forests other than old growth.[256]

The Forest Service announced a new policy on managing its forests. There would be fewer clear-cuts and longer rotations. The associate chief of the Forest Service, George M. Leonard, was quoted as saying that his guess was that over half the remaining old growth would be preserved.[257]

No matter the plans of Congress or the Administration, people on the ground still could not act, even if agreements had been reached. An editorial captured the essence of these acts and the frustrations generated.

"Maybe U.S. Congress members will learn what Pacific Northwest residents have learned about the preservationists: They can't be trusted. No sooner do they shake hands on a compromise agreement than they start breaking that agreement.

"The latest agree-then-renege example came just last week. President Bush affixed his signature to an Interior Department appropriations bill on Oct. 24 that included the compromise between the timber industry and the preservationists over the spotted owl and short-term timber supply. The compromise was reached after months of wrangling, threats, discussions, and uncertainty.

"Three days later, spokespersons for the Sierra Club, Audubon Society, Oregon Natural Resources Council and other environmental groups asked a judge to continue the lawsuit on behalf of the northern spotted owl and against old growth harvesting. The lawsuit has been on hold since May 26, pending the outcome of negotiations between lawmakers and preservationists over old growth. The signing of the appropriations bill was to have been the start of a 12-month truce agreed to by lawmakers, the timber industry and preservationists.

"The preservationists' word is no good. With this latest example of turnabout, maybe more congressmen will realize this fact, too." [258]

Other newspapers picked up the frustration theme. A business paper printed editorials from the Eugene *Register-Guard* and the Coos Bay *World.* The former said in part, "Politically and economically, this one-year deal (the Hatfield-Adams amendment) is fair, proper and practical. We hope the judge will find it capable of withstanding legal assault as well and tell the plaintiffs to be quiet and go away for at least a year." The latter said in part, "They (environmental extremists) have literally nit-picked the Forest Service and Bureau of Land Management to death; they have abused the appeals process to buy time, instead of finding resolutions." [259]

Environmentalists had filed separate lawsuits against the Forest Service and BLM. U. S. District Judge William Dwyer ruled that the action in

Congress allowing some timber harvest including old-growth trees was now constitutional and lifted the injunction in the Forest Service suit. There was hope that the Forest Service could move quickly to auction some timber. Plaintiffs argued that Congress acted unconstitutionally.[260] At the same time BLM was moving to have the lawsuit that was holding up their timber sales dismissed. Environmentalists, too, were opposing that action.[261]

Environmentalists initiated a study of the impact of reduced federal timber harvest on communities in federal timber dependent locations. Linn County, Rep. VanLeeuwen's district, was a major target of the study. The objective of the study was to plan how rural, timber-dependent towns could adjust to a cut in federal timber supply.[262]

In the meantime, environmentalists were being very clear about their goals. Howie Wolke wrote for the Earth First! organization a detailed set of goals. These were published under the title: EARTH FIRST! "BIOCENTRIC FORESTRY" VISION PLAN OUTLINED.[263]

The 17 goals were:

1. Repeal the Multiple Use-Sustained Yield Act, the Knutsen-Vandenberg Act, the National Forest Management Act.
2. Fire all Forest Service employees from the District Ranger level up. Reduce total agency employment by 75 percent.
3. Require all decision makers to be biologists.
4. Grant immediate protection to all roadless areas.
5. Designate two-thirds of the total National Forest Acreage as Wilderness.
6. Complete restoration of 100,000 miles of roads.
7. No new roads will be allowed in the future.
8. No off-road vehicles will be allowed in the designated areas.
9. No new ski areas or other large resorts will be allowed in these areas.
10. The Annual Timber Harvest level will be reduced by 90 percent.
11. No clearcutting will be allowed.
12. There will be no logging within 150 feet of riparian habitats; no herbicides, insecticides or fungicides will be used.
13. Extirpated native species will be reintroduced.
14. Domestic livestock grazing will be eliminated.
15. Natural, lightning-induced fires will be allowed to resume their historic role.
16. All remaining old growth forest will be protected.
Unnumbered. All human uses would be subservient to the primary purpose of protecting and restoring healthy ecosystems throughout the public lands."

National Forests were actively reducing the planned harvest. An *Evergreen* editorial, reproduced by a local paper, attempted to explain what was going on.[264] On the Rogue River National Forest, with an estimated annual growth of 190 million board feet, the plan being considered called for a harvest of 115 to 130 million board feet. This reduced cut was being planned in spite of the fact that local residents were pleading with the Forest Service to consider both preserving the forest while maintaining the local economy.

A district ranger tried to get local people to understand that the Forest Service was changing. In a talk to a forestry group the ranger reported, "Citizens who deal with the U. S. Forest Service should expect to see a different organization evolving over the next few years."[265]

At about the same time, Oregon State University scientists published an up-dated report on Oregon's timber production potential. Their prediction was that the forests of Oregon could produce on a sustained basis some 10 to 25 percent less than the peak volumes of the mid 1980s.[266]

What the national forests would do in response to the Hatfield-Adams Amendment remained to be determined. An advisory board consisting of a wide range of interests was appointed to advise the Willamette National Forest on how it should determine what stands should be selected to meet its quota of 680 million board feet in the coming year.[267]

Timber dependent counties in Oregon were being stressed in many ways by the reduced harvest of federal timber due to the efforts being made to protect the spotted owl. Among other stresses were the costs associated with legal challenges in courts to stop timber harvests. From whence should the money come? One suggested solution—use timber receipts. Counties that received federal money in lieu of taxes were asked to put 1.5 percent of their receipts into a fund with the Association of O & C Counties to help pay legal costs, an amount of approximately $1.6 million.[268]

Costs for wildlife and recreation management that had been absorbed by the Forest Service for nearly a century from its timber receipts were being faced head-on. The Wilderness Society was suggesting that the agency could make more money collecting recreation user fees than it could from timber sales.[269]

Meanwhile, biologists were still trying to tie down some basic biology of the spotted owl: habitat needs for breeding, nesting and feeding. Answers to those questions are important as the U. S. Fish and Wildlife Service considers the listing of the species.[270] Rep. Van- Leeuwen sent a letter to the papers in her district urging readers to write the USFWS protesting the listing of the owl, saying that nearly 3 million acres of federal land were already set aside for non-timber uses and that listing the owl would have devastating effects in her district.[271] Her concerns were increased with the news that more owls had been found on the Willamette National Forest. Although the news was not clear, these were found only in areas of potential timber harvest. The millions of acres set aside for other uses had yet to be surveyed.[272] To try to influence the decisions on federal land management grass roots organizations were forming and re-forming.[273]

The national press took note of the timber/owl controversy. Newsweek published a story by Shawn Doherty. The story quoted people from all sides of the argument and concluded with these paragraphs:

"Changing times: It has become clear that Sweet Home [and the Sweet Home Ranger District of the Willamette NF] and its rangers will have to forge a new kind of alliance in order to survive. Ranger Karen Barnette, whom skeptical townspeople dub "the lady ranger", took over the district this year to lead that effort. Barnette cheerfully admits she can't tell a tree's age from the rings in its stump—she majored in anthropology, not forestry—but she knows plenty about people, and changing ways of life. She warns townspeople at Kiwanis and Lions luncheons that they're going to have to use the area's woods and lakes to diversify into recreation and tourism. Rangers are also helping townspeople restore a covered bridge, and plan other potential tourist attractions, including a logging museum.

"Loggers snap their suspenders at such schemes. "We're timber people. That's all we know," says Skip Stock. "We don't want to run some bed-and-breakfast."

"But others in Sweet Home worry that the resumption of timber sales will give townspeople only a few more years to cut trees and curse the owl, but not enough time to get a new start. Sadly enough, it's easier to blame a bird than face one's own extinction." [274]

The president of the Chamber of Commerce responded:

"After reading the Newsweek article regarding Sweet Home and the timber industry problems, I'm not sure whether I feel angry, embarrassed or agree with the article. Perhaps the truth is, I feel a little of all three.

"I feel some anger in that the article, in my opinion, is very shallow and does not come close to describing the timber crisis, its causes and effects. This isn't really about owls. If the organizations filing suits over the owl were truly concerned with saving possibly threatened species, they would simultaneously push for protection of the other 10 animals on their list to use if they lose on the spotted owl issue. If they are endangered, why wait? Let's save them. Unless of course, there are other motives.

"But, once again, we are portrayed to the nation as only concerned with cutting all the trees and not caring about the environment. The article perpetrates the myth that in just a couple of years, our trees will be gone. And then, we're totally finished. Where is the part about forest management practices, reforestation, and enhancement of wildlife through the efforts of the public and private timber groups?

"I feel both anger and embarrassment that the death of a spotted owl south of here some months ago is virtually blamed on loggers. Now, I don't know who killed that owl. Maybe it was a logger and maybe it wasn't. But all of the "owl bashing" bumper stickers certainly point us out to the nation as the most likely to be guilty.

"I admit I had one on my pickup, too. But it's gone and has been for some time. Communities for a Greater Oregon has asked for several months that the negative stickers be removed. C.G.O. has a very good one to replace the bad ones. You can get one free by contacting C.G.O. at Sherman Supply Co.

"Then I feel anger and embarrassed to admit agreement with many of our problems came from logging practices of years past. If proper foresight and good forest management practices had been used then, some of our problems wouldn't exist today.

"But not-so-Sweet Home? Obviously the writer did not talk to any of the people I know. Yes, we've got problems. Yes, there are going to be changes in the timber industry. Yes, there is going to be some pain and suffering. But we have a powerful tool to fight back with and minimize and help direct the changes. And that tool is people. Their voices and votes. I don't believe Sweet Home is going to roll over and die. This is a tremendous town with a lot of good people. I'd like to invite the writer of the article back in about five years and let's see what's Sweet or not so Sweet."[275]

The president of the Chamber reflected the optimism of the time. Problems could be solved and the communities made whole again.

The decision to list or not list a species under the ESA does not have to be made in the light of economic or social consequences. Nevertheless, the state forester, James E. Brown, wrote to the Regional Director of the USFWS and pleaded with him to at least make a part of the record of decision the impact of listing the spotted owl would have on the forest industry and timber dependent communities in Oregon.[276]

The law of supply and demand was alive and working in the fall of 1989. After the Hatfield-Adams amendment became law, the Forest Service could begin selling timber. Purchasers knew that the supply was drying up. The result was higher and higher stumpage prices. For example, at the Sweet Home Ranger Station a timber company bid $1,567 per thousand board feet for prime Douglas-fir stumpage. The appraised price was $380.61.[277] In fiscal 1987 the Willamette National Forest led the nation in timber revenue. Such sales as the one in Sweet Home would help maintain that record.[278]

December 20, 1989 was the last day for commenting on the listing of the northern spotted owl as threatened under the ESA. Big guns on both sides of the controversy were still firing. The Wilderness Society, it was reported, said, "Spotted owl habitat in the Pacific Northwest is so severely decimated and fragmented that listing the owl as threatened is not merely justified but essential to the bird's survival." The Northwest Forest Resources Council, it was reported, said that, "Spotted owls are found in some young forests and highly fragmented stands of timber in numbers equal to or greater than those in old-growth forests." Continuing, the Council said, "The confirmed inventory of owls was more than 6,000." The USFWS was holding to an inventory number of 1,500 breeding pairs.[279]

At the same time timber sales by the Forest Service continued to bring record bids. Following the record of the day before, the Sweet Home District sold seven more sales at over twice the appraised value.[280] At the same time industry associations were reporting imminent danger for the industry due to reduced timber supply.[281]

Part of the timber compromise hammered out in Washington was the requirement that citizen advisory boards review sales by BLM and the Forest Service. The BLM had appointed such boards and worked through the reviews. For four of its district's sales, however, the Oregon Natural Resources Council challenged the sales in court. The agency said it would make the sales but not award them until the courts had ruled on the challenge.[282]

The year ended much as it had begun—in controversy and in court.

CHAPTER THIRTEEN

WINTER/SPRING 1990

The fate of the forests and the people in the timber dependent communities of the Pacific Northwest was an international question. The Oregon Natural Resources Council drew this quote from the London England *Times:*

"They are felling Oregon's glory, trunk by trunk. The majestic old trees 6 feet thick and soaring 200 feet into the blue northern sky have stood on these mountains since the discovery of America. Now they are crashing down in record numbers...disappearing at an equivalent of 86 football fields a day..."[283]

Following the quote the document goes on to say:

"Less than 10% of Oregon's original forestlands remain as ancient forests. Yet we continue to lose nearly 9 square miles of ancient forest each month."[2]

Rep. VanLeeuwen wrote to the Chief of the Forest Service, F. Dale Robertson, about her concerns for the management of the national forests and the spotted owl.[284] In her letter she emphasized:

"There are 4.2 million acres of old growth forest already permanently set aside in the states of Oregon and Washington. This area is equal to a strip of forest two miles wide, stretching across the continent from Portland, Oregon, to New York City!" This surely makes it impossible for the Northern Spotted Owl to run out of nesting area, or for the last 'ancient' tree ever to be cut." [3]

The representative refers to Wilderness areas in all national forests. In Oregon 2,072,020 acres have wilderness designation. In addition, another 932,838 acres are off limits to logging in national recreation areas, scenic areas, etc.[285]

This was a time when the USFWS was still considering the listing of the northern spotted owl under provisions of the ESA. All sides were attempting to get their point of view across. Environmentalists wanted timber harvest stopped on federal land, as we have seen previously. Legislators cared about constituents. The forest products industry was

---

[2] A football field is 50 yards wide and 100 yards long, or 50,000 square feet. There are 43,560 square feet in an acre. Eighty-six football fields would cover 98.71 acres, say 100. Using 30 days per month, then that would be 3,000 acres per month. There are 640 acres in a square mile. 3,000 divided by 640 equals 4.6875, the number of square miles per month being harvested, if the *London Times* is correct, not 9 square miles as the recruitment document asserts.

[3] Actually the strip would be more than 2 ½ miles wide.

supporting research into the biology of the owl. A brochure summarized some findings:

Early research misinterpreted

"Why is there such a difference of opinion regarding the true habitat needs of the northern spotted owl? It all stems from the misinterpretation of early research conducted on national forest lands managed by the U. S. Forest Service.

"These lands, which were partially harvested beginning in the 1940s, contain only two age classes of timber stands: one to 40 year-old plantations, and stands that are older than 200 years.[4]

"Spotted owls were found in both types of habitat, but in greater numbers in the old-growth stands. Because their numbers were greater in these stands, spotted owls were assumed to be 'dependent' on old growth.

"However, the lack of stands 50 to 200 years old in the study areas caused many researchers to question this conclusion.

"These questions provided the catalyst for additional studies now being conducted in Oregon, Washington and California which are providing new information—information the U. S. Fish and Wildlife Service has not considered.

"*Recent studies provide new information on the true habitat needs of the northern spotted owl*

"The best example of this new information, which is applicable to the entire Pacific Northwest, comes from three research projects conducted in northern California. These studies are being conducted on nearly one million acres of privately owned forestland that have been intensively managed for timber production since 1869.

"Most timber stands in the study area are 30 to 80 year old second-growth stands.

"Population surveys show that spotted owls have colonized these young timber stands in numbers comparable to those found in old-growth forests. During these surveys, scientists made over 400 owl sightings, including 75 breeding pairs living in second growth stands.

"This new research demonstrates beyond a doubt that spotted owls are not dependent on the age of trees for survival but on the existence of certain vegetative structures found throughout the Pacific Northwest.

True habitat needs of northern spotted owls

"Like any wildlife species, the northern spotted owl needs three things to survive: shelter; a food supply; and protection from predators.

"Shelter and nesting sites are provided by dead or dying trees. For food, the northern spotted owl depends on rodents and small mammals,

---

[4] This is true except for the stands that came in following fires that burned between 40 and 200 years ago. BBS.

which thrive in the presence of large, downed logs and other decaying material. A multi-layered canopy provides protection from predators.

"These vegetative structures are found not just in old growth ecosystems, but in many age classes of forest found in the Pacific Northwest, structures which can easily be created through management using existing practices.

"It can no longer be said that spotted owls are limited to preserved tracts of old growth for survival. By slightly modifying cutting practices, forests can be managed to maintain spotted owl habitat indefinitely, while continuing to allow forests to provide the nation with a sustainable level of timber production.

"As we have learned more about the biology of the northern spotted owl, we have developed new ways to manage forests to create biologically diverse habitats that will ensure the continuation of the species.

"We now know that there is no reason to list the northern spotted owl as threatened under the Endangered Species Act. Through research, understanding, and continuing proper management, the northern spotted owl will always have a home in the forests of the Pacific Northwest."[286]

This assessment of the spotted owl situation, as we look at it with 20-20 hindsight a decade later, is quite fair. That does not mean that all parties concerned accepted it.

The surveying on which the above pamphlet was based stimulated other private companies to initiate research. One such effort by Simpson Timber Co. found many owls in second growth forests in coastal northern California. The tentative working hypothesis was that because the second growth forests there were quite diverse and grew rapidly, the stands at 40 years of age had sufficient old growth characteristics to make them suitable northern spotted owl habitat.[287]

Observers from outside the forest industry/environmentalist community tried to bring rational discussion to the question of use wisely or preserve. An example was Warren Brooks, a nationally syndicated economics columnist. He wrote that he found much evidence for the benefits of forest management and little supporting the idea of preserving, i.e., not cutting, forests.[288]

Congress governs the management of natural resources on federal land in the West. Westerners have long had a minority position in Congress because of the allocation of seats in the House of Representatives on a population basis and because of the allocation of seats in the Senate based on two seats per state. States in the East are generally much smaller geographically than western states. The net result is that from a western perspective, outsiders exercise control of the management of natural resources.

Consider the case of Congressman Jim Jontz. Mr. Jontz came from Illinois. He was an environmentalist and was outspoken in his support for reduced timber harvests on national forests in the Pacific Northwest. In January 1990 he visited Oregon. In Curry County he met with Commissioners and timber people. It was reported: "Jontz's message to the local public officials and timber people was that federal timber sales are going to be reduced and there is nothing they can do about it." [289] Painful but true.

An oft-repeated statement about the forests of the Pacific Northwest is that they are the most productive in the world. Rarely does one hear that there is agreement on how much those forests can produce. Answers to questions about the level of sustainable production are couched in technical jargon that leaves the reader feeling numb. Within agencies, the debate went on. Internal BLM memos are an example. Environmental groups obtained copies of BLM memos that suggested that recent levels of harvest on BLM lands were too high, that such levels could not be sustained and that in the near future harvests would have to be reduced.[290]

The Hatfield-Adams Amendment directed that advisory panels be established on national forests to review proposed timber sales. The Willamette National Forest citizen's advisory panel, with seven members, had 150 possible timber sales on the Forest to review in the first six months of 1990. For each sale the panel could recommend for or against a sale. The recommendation on each sale went to the forest supervisor, who could accept or reject the panel's counsel. The headline for the report on the panel's meeting on Sweet Home and Detroit Ranger District sales captured the enormity of the undertaking: "Advisory panel takes on large task."[291]

The essence of these issues was crystallized in a letter from Rep. VanLeeuwen to a journalist at the *Christian Science Monitor*, John Hart. The Representative had known Mr. Hart when he lived in Corvallis, the son of a Baptist minister, and she was a student at Oregon State University. Her letter to Mr. Hart, pleading for even-handed coverage of natural resource issues, summarized the state of the forests as best she could in an unbiased manner. Basically her message was, "We know that the real issue is not the endangering of Northern Spotted Owls or the cutting of the last 'ancient' tree. The real issue is the management of our forest lands."[292]

And one way to manage those lands was to cease all timber harvest. The Oregon Natural Resources Council was explicit in that regard:

EUGENE (AP) - "The president of the Oregon Natural Resources Council says the environmental group is going to get tougher on opposing old growth forest harvests this year.

"Tom Giesen, a Eugene construction consultant, said in an interview Tuesday that the council's volunteer board members will assume more of a leadership role in the organization instead of relying so much on ONRC's paid staff. He said the ONRC has been perceived as what he called the 'Jim and Andy show,' referring to James Monteith, the group's executive director, and conservation director Andy Kerr.

"Board members also want to take a tougher stand on the old growth issue than staffers, Giesen said.

"'The staff has tended to be more moderate than the board on the old growth issue,' he said.

"Monteith said Tuesday that 'it's real nice when the board can be stronger, it makes my job a lot easier to have them pushing me.'

"'Clearly, this should not just be Monteith's idea of the way things ought to be done, or Kerr's idea of the way it should be done, or Wendell Wood's idea, either,' Monteith said. Wood is the group's Western Oregon representative based in Eugene.

"As part of the get-tough effort, the ONRC and the Ancient Forest Alliance, a coalition of environmental groups, is proposing federal legislation that would immediately halt all old growth logging.

"The proposal also would ban public log exports, tax private log exports, replace federal timber receipt payments with in-lieu-of-property-tax payments, fund worker relocation and retraining programs, provide incentives for adding high-value secondary manufacturing in Oregon, and transfer the U. S. Bureau of Land Management to the U. S. Forest Service.

"The plan is more restrictive than proposals offered recently by two large national environmental organizations, The Wilderness Society and the National Audubon Society.

"He said the two national groups might not have proposed their own old growth plans without pressure from the ONRC and other regional groups. 'There's just enormous grassroots pressure to get tough,' Giesen said.[293]

The same article concluded with a comment from the timber industry: "Ross Mickey, a spokesman for the North West Timber Association in Eugene, said he's glad the ONRC has finally 'stated what their real objectives are' in regard to halting old growth logging. 'Their actions all along have shown them to be hard line,' Mickey said. "He predicted economic disaster for the Northwest if any of the old growth protection plans become law."

The U. S. Forest Service strove to help communities make the adjustment to reduced timber harvest. For example, the Sweet Home Ranger District's recreation specialist had joined the Chamber of Commerce. At a meeting of the Chamber, the specialist, Mandy Cole, suggested, "We can be partners in development of recreation and tourism."[294]

Residents in timber dependent communities were acutely aware of the evolving management of federal land. An example is a letter to the editor from a resident in the North Santiam Valley.

Mother Nature versus man!

"Mother Nature came into the Pacific Northwest with a bang a couple of weeks ago, and the forests will never be the same. The South Breitenbush and the Breitenbush Gorge are no longer old-growth set-asides. They are leveled acreages that will never be harvested or replanted. It will take at least another 100 years for it to even begin to resemble what it once was, and without reforestation there is a chance that won't even happen.

"The deer and elk will disappear from this area for some time to come as they are not stupid animals and know that wind blown logs are dangerous. The spotted owls, for which this area was set aside, will no longer habitate here, but move on to another stand, possibly even a second-growth forest.

"Mother Nature is harsh in her wonders and man is not. Where Mother Nature destroys and lets things follow, man replenishes and nurtures. Mother Nature doesn't believe in preservation. But she does believe that the fittest will survive.

"Doesn't that make man the better environmentalist in his use of the logs and his reforestation practices.

"Some of Mother Nature's flurries will be utilized and replanted for the betterment of all of us. Too bad the Breitenbush can't have the same kind of treatment."[295]

Follow-up stories on the Willamette National Forest Advisory Panel revealed the disparate attitudes of the members. A representative of the forest industry said he was optimistic about the timber compromise. Members of the panel from environmental groups called the panels "a sham."[296]

Foresters are by their nature conservative people. It was not surprising, then, that foresters from BLM were trying to get permission to salvage some bug-killed timber on their land. "Officials from the BLM Medford District discussed the matter (logging bug-killed timber) Monday for four hours with officials of the Oregon Department of Fish and Wildlife, said BLM District forester Paul Kangas. They're going to go back and talk about it, he said." Further in the story it was reported that, "Last month, state wildlife officials turned down BLM's request for permission to salvage 8 million board feet of beetle-killed timber standing in spotted owl habitat areas in the Applegate area outside Medford. Wildlife officials turned down the request, saying standing dead trees are an important component of the old-growth forest habitat favored by the owls. 'We're still saying we think we can salvage that volume with minimal impact on the owl,' Kangas said."[297]

Subsequently BLM dropped its salvage plans. The agency announced that because of lack of support from state wildlife officials it was dropping plans to salvage standing dead timber from spotted owl zones in the Medford District. "It seems like logging in there would be a bit premature, when the question of whether the owl is going to be listed (as a threatened species) will be answered in the next several months," said Dan Carlson, a forest biologist for the Oregon Department of Fish and Wildlife.[298]

The tensions of the times were captured in a letter from the ranger on the Sweet Home Ranger District, Willamette N. F., to Rep. VanLeeuwen.
Date: February 13, 1990
"Honorable Liz VanLeeuwen,
27070 Irish Bend Loop,
Halsey, Oregon 97348

"Dear Rep. VanLeeuwen:
"Your letter of February 2 follows comments you made at the Albany Chamber of Commerce meeting January 26 and indicates serious concerns about land allocations proposed in the Willamette National Forest planning process. You also mention reservations about my actions as manager of the Sweet Home Ranger District. I believe there is always potential for misunderstanding and lack of communication when such broad activities as National Forest management are involved. I hope that I can provide answers to your questions and thus improve our communications.

"Each of us approaches the issues surrounding land and resource management from a slightly different perspective and naturally that affects our actions on any given issue. I can assure you that my actions do reflect my convictions and that my convictions regarding National Forest management center around 'caring for the land and serving people.' I am bound to reflect this within the laws and regulations which determine policy and provide a framework for setting direction for National Forest management.

"An important part of the Forest Service charge is that our management reflect 'the greatest good for the greatest number of people.' That means to me that the public I serve is a national one; Congress has dictated that the Forest Service take a national perspective in managing the land and resources within National Forest boundaries. While there continues to be a high demand nationally for wood products, as you point out, the demand for other types of goods and services from National Forest land has increased steadily over the past three decades. For many Forests within the National Forest system, balancing land and resource use indeed requires a shift in the historical management emphasis.

121

"Following are responses to some of your specific comments regarding land allocations in the current and proposed management plans for Willamette National Forest (WNF).

"1. You state that your information indicates WNF could '... sustain historic harvest levels and still protect the non-commodity values of the forest.' There are two points to consider in response. First, the harvest levels of the 1980's do not represent historic harvest levels, but an increase over those levels resulting primarily from the buy-out legislation of the early 1980's. This may have created unrealistic expectations. Second, the analysis done for the WNF Forest Plan does not support continued harvest at historic levels. This is due to a variety of factors, including legal safeguards for resource protection ranging from wildlife to watershed stability, and to the increasing demand for goods and services—including lands reserved from timber management—that I referred to previously. Not only have such restrictions and demands increased since the current plan was completed over a decade ago, but new information and research on resource condition and the impacts of management activities have dictated re-evaluation of the levels at which activities such as timber harvesting should occur.

"2. The current plan allocates 55% of the Forest to full yield timber harvest, 9% to timber harvest on a long rotation, and 36% to non-harvest status (your figures are essentially correct). The draft WNF Forest Plan drops the full yield harvest to 49% and the long rotation harvest to 7%, while increasing the no harvest category to 44%. The final Forest Plan is expected to decrease the full harvest allocation further, but not to the 32% level you quote. The decreases in full harvest and increases in no harvest acres are based on the factors I mentioned in (1), including a broad spectrum of public input. The Forest Service is certainly aware of the level of dependency of single resource economies; the Pacific Northwest Strategy is one attempt to recognize the historical dependency and help these communities manage the changes they are experiencing now and will continue to experience as the Forest Plans are implemented.

"3. Your figure of 67,700 acres refers to that portion of the released roadless areas within WNF which have been allocated to essentially undeveloped uses in the Forest Plan. The fact that these areas were released from further wilderness study through the roadless area review did not release the Forest Service from considering all the resource values present and making a final allocation recommendation based on resource protection considerations and a determination of the "highest and best" use in each case. The Forest has determined through the planning process and with consideration for public input that these acres should be left in an essentially undeveloped condition.

"4. With the exception of road number 15, all the roads you refer to are outside the Sweet Home Ranger District. In researching the change in visual quality objective (VQO) for road 15, I found that the change involved an extension of a partial retention area within the Blue River Ranger District. The other roads mentioned include Aufderheide Drive, which has been designated a national scenic byway. My impression is that the changes in VQO's for these roads were primarily the result of public input during the planning process. If you are interested in further information about these roads, I would suggest you contact Rolf Anderson, WNF Planning Officer based in the Supervisor's Office in Eugene, or the individual Ranger Districts in question.

"5. The final Forest Plan will recommend that some pine marten and pileated woodpecker special habitat areas be managed as you suggested, using longer rotations, partial cuts, etc. to maintain habitat. The Ranger Districts have determined which areas are suitable for such management on a case-by-case basis.

"Certainly timber industry representatives are concerned about the declining harvest levels. Most have an understanding of why the decline is occurring, but question the amount of the decrease. Their questions are appropriate and the concern at all levels and in all arenas is real. I don't believe anyone in the Forest Service takes such concerns lightly. In fact, I think there is in general agreement that the Forest Service needs to take more of a leadership role in land and resource conservation. (*On her copy the representative wrote "or preservation???")*

"However, it is important to remember that the Forest Service mission, as established in its Organic Act of 1897, addresses three basic purposes for establishment of National Forests: to improve and protect the forest within the boundaries; to secure favorable conditions of water flows; and to furnish a continuous supply of timber for citizens of the United States. In carrying out this mission the Forest Service has numerous impacts, both beneficial and adverse, on communities within its sphere of influence. I believe we are obligated not to maintain community stability, but to recognize the effects of Forest Service decisions on communities, particularly timber-dependent communities, and assist those communities in whatever way possible in developing viable economies. The Forest Service should not in any case attempt to dictate a community's future, but should respond to needs and opportunities which the community itself has developed. Once again, I believe this is what the Pacific Northwest Strategy is all about.

"I am enclosing a vision statement and a press release about the Pacific Northwest Strategy. Very little has been written, as it is still primarily a concept and very loose as to what specific actions will occur to carry out the strategy. I can tell you that it is not a Forest Service initiative. Although the idea originated in the Forest Service Regional Office in Portland, the steering committee is made up of individuals from a broad spectrum of state and federal government entities, private industry, and the academic community (see the list of members on the back of the yellow vision statement). To me, the possible activities are not new, but include a variety of actions that have been taking place at the ground level for many years. In a sense, the Pacific Northwest Strategy validates the Forest Service role in assisting resource- dependent communities in maintaining or developing viable economies.

"I am also enclosing a copy of a White House press release dated 1/22/90 which outlines a Presidential initiative on rural development and implements a report from the White House Economic Policy Council's Working Group on Rural Development. The report is attached. I hope you will find it interesting. Note that the report goes beyond a focus on agriculture-dependent communities to discuss resource-dependent communities in general and the appropriate federal agency relationship to those communities.

"I would welcome the opportunity to talk to you more about any of the issues discussed above. I would particularly like to discuss further the Pacific Northwest Strategy and the Sweet Home Ranger District's program as it relates to that strategy. The Linn Tourism Coalition, which you mention in your letter, is an example of the type of activity which the Strategy encourages, although the seeds of that particular effort were planted before I arrived at Sweet Home or the term "Northwest Strategy" had been coined.

"I hope that this information is useful to you. I very much want to maintain open communications and give you the clearest understanding possible of Forest Service management activities, especially as they affect the area which you represent. Please do not hesitate to contact me at any time. "

Signed: Karen Barnette, District Ranger[299]

I have not discussed this letter with Rep. VanLeeuwen. In retrospect it must have been devastating. It was clear, unequivocal evidence that the management of national forests was no longer going to be primarily devoted to timber production. The vision statement and press release about the Pacific Northwest Strategy is not at hand, but it must have laid out even more the reality of reduced timber harvest. And for Rep. VanLeeuwen that spelled problems for her constituents.

Three days after the Barnette letter, in a letter dated Feb. 16, 1990, to the Chief of the Forest Service, F. Dale Robertson, Rep. VanLeeuwen said, "It was a pleasure to meet with you during my September trip to Washington, D. C. While there, in your office, 2000 miles removed from

Linn County, Oregon, we were able to objectively address the Northwest's timber issues. However, here in the heart of timber country, I find it especially important to remain objective, when it's so apparent that new policy coming from the U. S. Forest Service is not objective. The new policy leans heavily toward the 'preservationists' camp and is obviously, in my opinion, not based on objective data readily available. According to current available data, <u>the Willamette National Forest could sustain historical harvest levels and still protect the non-commodity values of the forest</u>. Thus I must conclude the timber harvest is slated to decrease, not because it is necessary, but because Forest Service officials are feeling pressured to do so. I conclude then, that the decision is political, not reasonable or in the best interest of anyone except the 'preservationists'."

She goes on later in the letter to say, "I urge you to base your decisions for our area on facts from reliable sources. Please help us <u>maintain</u> a balanced, sustained use of our forest lands." [300]

Evergreen carried an editorial by Troy Reinhart that recounted the story of Andy Stahl's report to the Sixth Annual Public Law Conference at the University of Oregon on March 5, 1988. From that he went on to review actions of federal agencies that seemed suspect regarding the northern spotted owl. He concludes with, "At long last Mr. Stahl's 'story' is catching up with him. We are left to wonder whether Congress or the U. S. Fish and Wildlife Service will continue to tolerate this sort of misuse of its legal, political and scientific processes. We hope not. There is too much at stake, economically and environmentally, to allow this sort of defiance and indifference for truth to persist."[301]

The timber sales authorized by the Hatfield-Adams Amendment were not going well. The advisory committee for the BLM in southwestern Oregon advised against sales that BLM proposed. The rejection was based on the idea that the timber harvest would have a serious impact on owl habitat.[302]

The pending decision on listing of the owl was generating much interest. The leaders of four federal agencies that manage land in the West met in Portland to consider the up-coming report of the scientific panel on the status of the northern spotted owl.[303] Lawmakers were concerned. In a story with a Washington, D. C. dateline, Representative Peter A. DeFazio, D-OR, was quoted as saying, "I feel like I'm on board the Titanic. We are headed for a disaster." The story went on to say, "DeFazio is worried because timber land in the Pacific Northwest is caught between conflicting increases in demand and decreases in supply."[304]

Congressman Robert F. Smith, R. OR, 2nd Dist., sought to shore up Representative VanLeeuwen's spirits in a letter. He quoted an Oregon Natural Resources Council newsletter that gave details of a bill in Congress to eliminate all natural resource extraction activity on federal land. The

Congressman assured the Representative that he would work to see the bill did not get passed.[305]

Reduced timber harvest on federal land was having an impact on Rep. VanLeeuwen's constituents. She sent out a "Dear Friends" letter that told of a mill shutdown and a shift cancellation in another mill, both in Sweet Home. She included information on where out-of-work people could get support and gave addresses of congressmen to whom they should write telling of their hardships.[306]

Reality was setting in in other places. The local paper in Lebanon, OR said, in part, "Decision time is coming regarding the spotted owl and listing it as an endangered species…[I]t looks as if we are going to have to put aside even more timber land for the owl whether we like it or not, whether it costs jobs or not, or whether it is fair or not."

A decision on listing was due in late June 1990.

CHAPTER FOURTEEN

CRUNCH TIME

APRIL, MAY and JUNE 1990

The Federal Register[5] for June 26, 1990, said, in part, "SUMMARY: The U. S. Fish and Wildlife Service (*Service*) determines the northern spotted owl (*Strix occidentalis caurina*) to be a threatened species pursuant to the Endangered Species Act of 1973, as amended (*Act*)." This action was the culmination of a steadily intensifying debate over the status of the owl and the impact the listing of the owl might have on Oregon and the Pacific Northwest. The record of the debate can be viewed in many ways. In what follows we follow the debate in the press, in correspondence among politicians, in letters to editors, in industry pronouncements, in governmental reports, and in environmental organization declarations in chronological order during the three months leading up to the listing decision.

THE PRESS

The opening salvo in this final period came on April 3, 1990. Under this headline: "Many await owl report due out Wednesday" was a story with a Washington dateline by the Associated Press. The story summarizes the situation in a succinct way:

"Several hundred U. S. forest Service employees are among those who hope a scientific report[6] will recommend radical changes in timber cutting plans to protect the northern spotted owl.

"The interagency report, to be released Wednesday, will be reviewed during a special joint hearing. The House Agriculture Subcommittee on Forests, Family Farms and Energy, and the Interior and Insular Affairs Subcommittee on National Parks and Public Lands will meet on the report.

"Environmentalists want the owl listed as an endangered species, but critics of the effort say it could cripple the Pacific Northwest's economy by reducing by half the amount of timber logged in the region's national forests.

"The Association of Forest Service Employees for Environmental Ethics asked Congress in a recent letter to enact a moratorium on logging and development in any remaining old-growth forests.

"Jeff DeBonis, president of the Eugene-based group and a former Forest Service worker at Willamette National Forest, said the Forest Service is, "failing in its mission to protect and manage" public lands.

---

[5] Volume 55, No. 123, pages 26114-26194.
[6] This refers to the Interagency Scientific Team or the Thomas Report.

"'Right now, our national forests are not being managed in an ecologically sustainable manner, and will continue to be degraded in a non-sustainable manner even under most of the new forest plans,' he said.

"The congressional hearing scheduled for Wednesday will offer the first public glimpse of the scientific panel's report on the status of the northern spotted owl.

"The U. S. Fish and Wildlife Service, which will decide in June whether to list the owl as threatened or endangered, extended its comment period this month just so it could receive the panel's recommendation.

"The committee, led by Forest Service biologist Jack Thomas, met in Portland last month with Forest Service chief F. Dale Robertson, Bureau of Land Management director Cy Jamison, John Turner of the Fish and Wildlife Service and Jim Ridenour of the National Park Service.

"Robertson said following that meeting he expects the panel will recommend the Forest Service ban logging in more old-growth forests to protect the owl. He told Congress, in recent weeks, if the owl is declared endangered it could reduce cuts in national forests by 30 percent to 50 percent.[307]

"Scientists: Cut logging to save owl" blared a headline.[308] The story began, "Logging must stop across a large section of national forests in the Pacific Northwest to keep the northern spotted owl from moving toward extinction, a government panel of scientists said today."

A day later this headline: "Owl report called 'catastrophic'" The lead paragraph continued, "Stunned timber industry representatives predict economic catastrophe if the government follows the recommendations of top government scientists to drastically reduce the harvest of old growth timber in the Northwest."[309]

The public, as represented by the press, had difficulty understanding some of the basic biology of the northern spotted owl. An editorial examined the descriptions of the preferred forest of the owl and concluded that the forests being saved were poor and potentially dangerous forests. The conclusion was based on the Interagency Scientific Team's description of the habitat preferred by the owl: "Habitats selected by northern spotted owls typically exhibit moderate to high canopy closure; a multilayered, multispecies canopy dominated by large overstory trees; a high incidence of large trees with large cavities, broken tops, and other indications of decadence; numerous large snags; heavy accumulations of logs on the forest floor; and considerable open space within and beneath the canopy." [310]

"Managed Forests Last Forever," said a placard held by a woman attending a rally in Portland and pictured on the front page of the Eugene Register Guard.[311] The rally was held to protest the plan for the spotted owl. It was estimated that 10,000 people, millworkers and loggers and their families, were in attendance. The people had come from all over western Oregon.

Editorials supported the rally and the people who made up the crowds. Under "A Job Well Done" banner the Sweet Home paper editorialized: "By any standard of measurement, Sweet Home deserved an 'A' for its part in Friday's 'Jobs—Not Handouts' timber rally in Portland. When one considers it came about after only four days of intensive grassroots planning, its success is astounding." [312]

Rightly or wrongly, the anticipated ruling was being framed as a decision between owls and jobs. This led to questions about the purpose of national forests. An editorial examined the historical roots of the national forests. Gifford Pinchot, it was noted, had said, "You will see to it that the water, wood and forage of the reserves are conserved and wisely used for the benefit of the home builder first of all, upon whom depends the best permanent use of lands and resources alike." The editorial opined that the forests would not have been established in 1905 if the Congress then had known that some 85 years later "might be all but closed to sensible forestry because of a subspecies of owl." [313]

The estimates of harvest reductions to come were having an immediate impact on the forest products industry. For example, "Three mills closing down in mid-valley" was a headline. The story reported on mills closing due to lack of raw material and other causes. [314]

"Now it's about the owl" was the headline for an editorial about owls and jobs. "Now that the impact of the northern spotted owl is beginning to sink in, it is obvious that it would have been far better to avoid a showdown over what federal law requires to protect a single rare species. That's what the Fish and Wildlife Service under the Reagan administration had in mind, but its critics and the courts would not let it. " The editorial went on to discuss what had become a conflict over owl protection and an estimated loss of 15,000 family wage jobs. It concluded with, "If only the courts had respected the earlier decision against listing the owl as endangered, political though it might have been, and had let that decision stand!" [315]

In a similar vein, "Owl estimate important—it's from governor" pointed out that there were two reasons the announcement from the governor's office was important regarding the Thomas report. "First, because of the numbers involved, and, secondly, because of who issued the information." "The governor's report said the owl plan would cost Oregon 15,400 jobs and $610 million in lost salary and wages by 1995." [316]

According to the lead article in the Eugene paper protecting the owl carries a big price tag. [317] The article was more specific than others. It reported job losses and reductions in timber sales from federal forests, a drop in timber receipts and the drop in payments to Oregon schools and counties. The message was the same. Big drops.

The Portland *Sunday Oregonian* [318]reported on a telephone poll that found that 60% disagreed with the statement "To protect the spotted owl, we would stop logging on large tracts of federal timberland as recommended by the recent federal study, even if it means a loss of jobs." Six hundred people were polled.

The impact of reduced timber harvest to protect the northern spotted owl extended beyond the immediate families involved. Payments to counties, from timber harvests on federal land in which the forests are located, support schools and county services. This fact was pointed out in an editorial titled, "Saving owl seen as threat to schools."[319]

A full page advertisement in the Eugene paper funded by the Willamette Forestry Council, Inc. of Creswell, OR had a banner headline: "Fairness in Forest Management." A map of owl reserves in the Cascades and Coast Ranges showed the extent of land being taken out of the timber base. A table showed the economic impact of the owl in the Northwest. The figures were: harvest reduction of 1.8 billion board feet, which translated into $1.86 billion dollars annually. That harvest reduction, prorated, came to $2.07 million dollars for each pair of owls.[320]

The possibility of listing the owl was impacting timber sales on the national forests. For example, the headline, "Concern for owls stops two timber sales" was spread across the front page of the Albany paper.[321] The sales were in mostly old growth timber and the fear was that somehow, if the trees were cut, it would be impossible for the owls to move north/south in that section of the Cascades. Some 10.4 million board feet were in the sales.

The BLM joined the U. S. Forest Service in stopping or delaying sales in areas that might be declared owl habitat.[322] It was preparing management plans for its land in western Oregon and hoped to have them completed by 1992. In the meantime, efforts were being made to keep as many options open as possible.

The day of decision was at hand. On June 23, 1990 the Albany paper ran four stories related to the owl that almost filled a full page. The first[323] described how the U. S. Fish and Wildlife Service would subsequently have final say on whether U. S. Forest Service or BLM could cut old growth forest. The second[324] reported on Eric Forsman's experience with the owl. It was he who began studying the owl as a graduate student in the 1970s. He said, "It was a species that had received almost no attention. Everything you found was new, and it was a lot of fun." After all the study that had gone into the owl and the many estimates of the impact of saving the owl, there was much uncertainty. The third story reported on interviews with Northwest congressmen in Washington, D. C.[325] No one was sure what the impact would be until after the Forest Service and BLM announced their plans for saving the owl. The final story,[326] told how concerned Oregon's Governor Goldschmidt was about the impact on Oregon's economy. He said, "We must prevent that impact from being devastating to those communities and our state."

The conflict between the Endangered Species Act and society was neatly summarized in an editorial. The editor, Hasso Hering, said, "There has been a good deal of rhetoric about 'science' in the controversy about the spotted owl, which the government has now declared a threatened species. Two points demand to be made:

"Government officials have told the country what science supposedly says without disclosing details of the evidence or subjecting the evidence to critical review in the public arena. Right away, the "science" of the owl report is suspect, or at least open to question.

"Even if the scientific findings completely support the listing of the owl, science alone cannot be allowed to dictate what is done as a result. That's not how things are done in a democracy."

Later in the editorial Mr. Hering says, "What society does in response to scientific findings is determined not by science itself but, properly, by politics." Then he quotes Senator Hatfield, "We have the science with the Thomas report. Now we have to plug in the economic impact, the social impact, the educational impact, the tax impact, and all of the other factors in order to come up with a recovery plan."

The final paragraph of the editorial was, in retrospect, prescient:

"Never before has the Endangered Species Act been applied on such a large scale. Biology and other sciences certainly have an important role in carrying out this law. But if the effects of the owl listing on communities and people are played down or ignored, unelected government appointees will be accorded far more power in this country than they should have." [327]

THE POLITICIANS

Oregon's senior senator wrote to an officer in Pope and Talbot, a pulp mill in Halsey, OR, about his concerns and expectations. He said,

"Dear Mr. Sinclair:

"Thank you for contacting me recently about the spotted owl and the management of our national forests. I appreciate your taking time to offer some of you thoughts on this matter.

"As you may know, a special interagency scientific committee (known as the "Thomas Committee" (after Dr. Jack Ward Thomas, the biologist who chaired it) released a plan in early April 1990 which recommended the set-aside of nearly 8.4 million acres of forest lands for use as "habitat conservation areas" (HCAs) for the spotted owl. The plan focused on the biological needs of the owl, since the Thomas Committee's responsibility was to develop a plan, which would assure a viable population of owls "well distributed throughout its range." The Committee was not asked to consider economic factors in developing its plan.

"The day the Thomas Plan was released, I expressed my deep concern about the potential economic and social effects on Oregonians, indeed upon all Pacific Northwesterners, if the plan were adopted as recommended. In fact, I immediately requested assessment of the potential economic impacts of this plan. This assessment is being conducted on a number of fronts. We have just received the Bush Administration's assessment of the Thomas Plan's economic impact on the Pacific Northwest. That assessment shows a loss of 28,000 jobs regionally, and I find that number completely unacceptable.

"Additionally, the State of Oregon released just last week its final version of the Beuter update, which estimates 1.2 bbf, $640 million in personal income, and 15,400 total jobs lost in Oregon alone if the plan were adopted. Governor Goldschmidt has requested a more detailed evaluation of the effects of this plan if it were adopted as recommended, and this should be done by June 15th.

"We have also asked the federal resources management agencies to evaluate alternatives to the Thomas Plan which would provide protection for our ecologically significant old growth forest and for the spotted owl without having such a devastating impact on our federal timber sales program. Those alternatives are being prepared now, and should be presented to Congress roughly the same time the agency economic assessments are presented.

"Because there are so many questions about the assumptions and conclusions of the Thomas Plan, I have requested, and the Chairman of the Senate Energy and Natural Resources Committee has granted, an oversight hearing to review the Thomas Plan. The purpose of this hearing, to be conducted on May 23, 1990 in Washington, D. C., is to pose questions about the plan to the heads of the natural resources management agencies and to Dr. Thomas. These questions will not be posed because I question the credibility of Dr. Thomas and his committee. In fact, I believe the Thomas Committee performed its task with distinction.

"However, because of the critical importance to make informed and defensible policy decisions, the public has a right—and the Congress has an obligation—to understand the Thomas Plan and its underlying assumptions as thoroughly as possible before we proceed. We expect answers to our questions to be returned to the Committee in a timely manner so that the hearing record can be submitted to Secretary of the Interior Lujan for his consideration prior to the June 23rd deadline for making a listing decision for the owl.

"This is one of the most vexing problems I have faced in my 40 years of service to Oregon. It is very troubling that this matter has become so polarized and politically charged. I am confident, however, that we will be able to develop a balanced solution to this problem that reduces the political polarization, which currently characterizes this issue, and protects the livelihoods of Oregon's forest products workers, and protects the survival of the spotted owl. Your interest and continued input will aid us in that important effort.

"Kind regards.

"Sincerely.

Signed/ Mark O. Hatfield
United States Senator"[328]

It was becoming clear that if the owl were listed more than federal or state land would be impacted. Les AuCoin, an Oregon representative, expressed the concern of many when he noted, "This may be the first time it has been made so inexplicably clear that the habitat recovery plans...would affect private lands as well as public lands."[329]

The Oregon attorney general, Dave Frohnmayer, called for a cross examination of sorts of the biologists who recommend listing the northern spotted owl.[330]

As time went on, politicians were becoming more and more concerned about the impact the listing of the owl would have on their constituents. At the Washington level, Oregon's Senator Bob Packwood was reported to be unwilling to protect the spotted owl with a plan costing 13,400 jobs and affecting another 20,000 family members.[331] Rep. Les AuCoin was concerned that the listing could trigger a recession.[332] Rep. Denny Smith was suspicious that the job losses due to the owl listing might be higher than predicted.[333]

During a visit to Portland, President George Bush said that preserving jobs in Oregon's timber industry was as important as environmental concerns.[334] Rep. VanLeeuwen wrote the President and thanked him for coming to Oregon and expressing concern for the families in the timber dependent communities. She attached to her letter information on the forest situation in Oregon and insisted that the forests could support both the owl and the people.[335] Her primary thought was that multiple use of public land is the answer.

The Oregon governor, Neil Goldschmidt, said that protecting the spotted owl "will have a significant effect on the economy of many Oregon communities."[336]

But the pleas of the politicians went for naught. The owl was listed on June 23, 1990.

THE ENVIRONMENTALISTS

The environmentalists were watching the federal agencies closely to see what impact the compromise of the Timber Summit was having on the owl. The National Audubon Society released a report that said that two thirds of the sales planned on western Oregon national forests violated the compromise.[337]

They were also interacting with those with information about studies and reports being done and prepared by federal biologists. The conservation director for Oregon Natural Resources Council made public his information about the Thomas Committee report that was due.[338] He said that the set asides for the owl would be four million acres, which was about three times as much as the Forest Service and BLM had reserved for the owl. The article goes on to report that Thomas would neither confirm nor deny the report. He was quoted as saying, "Our professional ethics preclude release of any information in any report prior to its being in its final form. The people on my committee are all ethical professionals. I despise this stuff." Apparently Kerr had access to someone who knew of the report's contents or to a copy of the report. There is a summary of a report dated April 2, 1990, a Monday, that supports Kern's assertions.[339] A spokesman for a timber group suggested that it was probably a ploy for Kerr to get the information out prior to the publication of the report. He said if the final report showed lower numbers it could be claimed that timber people had brought pressure on the Thomas Committee.

The Oregon Natural Resources Council was soliciting funds to support its conservation and preservation efforts. The Lebanon *Express* used the copy it received to frame an editorial on the owl question.[340] Quotes from the letter were typical for such a letter and the editorial did a point-counterpoint to express the opinion that with such letters being sent out it was really easy to see why so few people appeared to be concerned about the plight of timber dependent communities.

The surveillance of timber sales planned as a result of the Timber Summit continued. A report claimed that 82 percent of the owl habitat would be destroyed. A BLM spokesman defended the sales saying that logging was prohibited while there were young owls present and that they could move to other areas and not be destroyed.

The Lebanon *Express* continued to press the case against environmental groups. In an editorial[341] the salaries, all at least six figures, of six prominent leaders of environmental organizations were listed. The editorial concluded with, "Makes you wonder what these gentlemen really care about, doesn't it?"

An Associated Press story with a Washington, DC,[342] dateline was typical of stories for the time regarding timber. It reported that environmental leaders had an audience in the White House on the spotted owl issue and that the leaders felt they had been well received. The story went on to add information from the Forest Service and projections on what the job losses might be to protect the owl. "It (the audience) gave us a chance to debunk some of the numbers that the timber industry has been using to support their case," Larry Tuttle, director of the Wilderness Society in Oregon, said.

THE PEOPLE

Rural Oregonians are not reluctant to write letters to politicians and newspapers expressing their opinion. Reading the letters a decade after they were written is a poignant experience.

Kevin R. Williams, Oregon City, OR, wrote to President George Bush.

"I am a native Oregonian and proud to be employed in our timber industry. However, our timber industry is now in grave danger, as is Oregon's economy

"If the Spotted Owl is listed as endangered, and the timber harvest is reduced, my family's sole support could be eliminated. All Oregonians have a lot to lose.

"Diversify you say? I have done so three times. Each job was lost because of the influence of the environmentalists. I was forced into bankrupcy (sic): I lost my home, my vehicles and my good credit standing. When my wife and I both found full-time employment, the bank refused our request to make double payments on our home to bring it current. We lost our home after ten years of making payments. The bank didn't seem to care!

"So what will you do with the thousands who may lose their jobs because of an owl? Shall we diversify, so our jobs can be taken again every time the environmentalists get a wild hair? Think of the schools, counties, and businesses that may fail without timber support. Think of the burden placed on the taxpayers of the Pacific Northwest, specifically, Oregon.

"When will America wake up to the reality of this devastation brought on by the environmentalists?! How many people have to lose their jobs and homes…How many families must feel the pain and humiliation that I suffered and may be forced to once again? - WHAT WILL IT TAKE FOR AMERICA TO REALIZE THAT THESE POWER-HUNGRY ENVIRONMENTALISTS HAVE GONE TOO FAR?!

"Please take a firm stand for Oregon's economy. Take a stand for timber!!

> Respectfully yours,
> S/ Kevin R. Williams"[343]

The president of a company in Hood River, OR had a suggestion.[344] "I am hereby declaring the month of May to be 'Timber Month,' and during the month of May I am sending a letter, in lieu of payment, to every company with which I do business and currently have a balance due on account. I am also refraining from purchasing anything but the bare, minimal essentials during this month. I believe our voices will be heard only if the forest products workers unite in a silent protest such as this."

An insurance man in Corvallis, OR wrote an open letter to President Bush, Oregon's two senators, Rep. Smith, Gov. Goldschmidt, and the secretaries of Interior and Agriculture.[345] He concluded his letter, which protested the shut-down of the timber industry, with these words: "Let's stop this silly excuse that a few have promoted so well without being cross-examined and made to prove—without a shadow of a doubt—that the spotted owls need that many millions of acres to fly around and over." The Thomas report had recommended 8.3 million acres of habitat to protect the owl.

Rep. VanLeeuwen received a letter from a man in Mapleton, OR, which is outside her district.[346] He told how he had worked his way through college, raised a family, worked hard and invested in timberland. He went on to say, "Hopefully you are aware of the present recommendations for set aside areas (HCAs) for the Spotted Owl. It so happens that our 111.32-acre parcel falls within one HCA and the 45.77-acre parcel is immediately adjacent to one. If the owl is listed as threatened or endangered on June 23, 1990, and the scientific study-recommendations are accepted by Congress, then our land within the HCA will be unusable regarding timber harvest, woodlot cutting, etc." Later, he continued," The rights of the private landowner are diminishing rapidly and that private land is being taken, subtly, without compensation."

A sense that something was not right with the owl science was reflected in letters. One, handwritten, said:
"Dear Liz

"Several years ago there was a spotted owl in the back of our place on Weirich Dr. in Lebanon. There is no old growth timber here it is all 2nd and 3 growth. We think there was a pair but only saw one at a time. There is 4 people that saw it at different times. There was a spotted owl found dead in our neighbors place. There were lots of chipmunks & squirrels here but when the owl was here they all disappeared and we have only saw one chipmunk since. We also saw a spotted owl a couple of years ago along the road going from Lebanon to Brownsville. There is not old growth timber around there either. The spotted owl has also been seen in the Tillamook Burn and there is no old growth timber there either. We have heard they are logging the Tillamook Burn again.

"It makes Dan mad to have the people burn the flag or tramp on it after he fought for it in World War 2.

"We will try to come over on June 24th if something don't come up so we can't come. We are on S. S. and cannot afford to call the President.

Sincerely,
S/ Mr. Mrs. Dan Usher"[347]

Under a headline "Costly Science," the Albany paper published a letter that questioned the science of the spotted owl report. It said:

"Earth Day 1990 has brought to mind some predictions of the first Earth Day in 1970: 'By 1985 air pollution will have reduced the amount of sunlight reaching the Earth by one half.' 'In the 1980s a major ecological system—soil or water—will break down somewhere in the U. S.' 'In a decade, urban dwellers will have to wear gas masks to survive air pollution.' LIFE magazine also said 'scientists have solid experimental and theoretical evidence' to support each prediction.

"None of these predictions by scientists have come true.

"Now we have another scientific report, the Jack Ward Thomas Report on the spotted owl. This report recommends setting aside 350 billion board feet of old-growth timber on 5 million acres of land managed by the Forest Service and Bureau of Land Management and Oregon Department of Forestry. This is in addition to the existing owl habitat areas already protected.

"Private landowners are not exempt. They too will be brought down under new regulations.

"Over 60,000 people will be put out of work in the northwest. Most of those 60,000 support a family—so the circle of hunger and homeless grows.

"Are we going to accept another 'scientific' study at this great cost? Please, let us think twice before we allow such devastation to our state.

S/ Geri McCloud, Lebanon, OR"[348]

The impact of that listing could only be guessed. Speculation varied widely, but not the actual consequences.

CHAPTER FIFTEEN

THE AFTERMATH—1990-2002

The owl was listed as threatened in June 1990. What began as a graduate student's thesis project in the late 1970s had resulted in the action by USFWS to list as threatened the northern spotted owl. The pleas and protestations of press, politicians and the people could not deter the agency, despite the solid evidence that the owl was actually not in jeopardy.

After the decision in June 1990, many people of good will tried to soften the blow of the shut-down of timber harvest on federal land. Despite the assurances of the agencies that there would be minimal reductions, by the year 2000 the annual cut on federal lands continued to decline. As President Clinton wound up his eight years in the While House the Forest Service was declaring another 60 million acres of roadless area off limits to all but minimal forest operations.[349]

In July 1990 Jack Ward Thomas, who headed the interagency scientific team that developed the owl plan, told a congressional hearing "that he hoped others would find innovative ways to meet the requirements of the Endangered Species Act and the National Forest Management Act that will ease the impact on the timber industry." "However," he continued, "having struggled for six months with some very qualified people, we could not find such a mechanism."[350]

Professor Robert Lee, University of Washington sociologist and student of forest dependent communities, described the impact on timber dependent communities:

"Losing jobs in timber communities means 'a loss of a way of life for people who see themselves as tough, resilient and proud, the people who built America,' Lee said.

"He said vilification of loggers by those on the other side of the issue is a form 'blaming the victims.'

"And there likely will be 'a sense of abandonment and betrayal,' he said, because sustain-yield timber production policies adopted by government encouraged wood products workers to put down roots in their communities.

"'Assumptions of easy adjustments are wrong,' Lee said. 'A temporary timber crisis we're in now can generate a permanent rural crisis.'

"'Depression, cynicism and even delayed stress syndrome like that suffered by some Vietnam War veterans could be among the effects of widespread job layoff,' Lee said.[351]

Rep. VanLeeuwen had written to Secretary of Interior Manuel Lujan pleading for an evidentiary hearing before the decision was made to list the owl. About a month after the decision was made the secretary wrote to the representative explaining that good people had done lots of work and that there was really no need for such a hearing.[352] After the explanation, he added, "Plans for protection of this species can build upon a variety of coordination and investigation efforts that have been undertaken over the past year. As a result of these efforts, I believe there is an immediate prospect for an orderly and uninterrupted flow of timber from the Pacific Northwest through the remainder of this fiscal year, and mechanisms are in place to promote effective cooperation among Federal agencies and with State and private interests in coming years."

Rep. VanLeeuwen's district included most of Linn County, OR. She obtained from Oregon Labor Trends employment figures for the county and state in the timber industry. She reported these employment figures:[353]

DATE	Linn County	State
January 1978	5490	
January 1979		78,500
January 1980	5260	74,000
January 1981	4920	
January 1987		64,600
January 1988	4950	67,600
January 1989	4330	67,500
January 1992	3670	53,400

The comparable data for 2000:[7]

	3340	47,700

There has been a reduction in the amount of timber sold on national forests and BLM land. Data from NFA Timber Facts, May 1999 are:

VOLUME UNDER CONTRACT—MMBF[8]

YEAR	USFS Volume	BLM Volume
1988-92 Annual Average	5,268	1,152
1997	1,092	362
1998	1,125	467
3/31/1999	1,072	434

Unfortunately, the status of the northern spotted owl is less clear. A September 1997 report by Bruce G. Marcot and Jack Ward Thomas sought to bring the matter up to date. The authors trace the history of the owl issue in detail. They offer insight into how management of federal timberland was affected. For example, on page 10, they show we have gotten into the gridlock over other, less obvious species:

---

[7] Provided by former Rep. VanLeeuwen in January 2001.
[8] MMBF = Million Board Feet.

"Anticipating that circumstances were likely to lead eventually to a demand to examine life forms other than vertebrates, the Scientific Advisory Team asked for and received permission to extend the assessment to all life forms of macroorganisms. This was a significant step toward a broader ecological basis for evaluating ecosystems."

This action in 1992 was the beginning of the idea of ecosystem management that included the "Survey and Manage" requirement for all these macroorganisms. The Forest Service's failure to do the surveys led to more environmental lawsuits.

The Marcot and Thomas report contains an interesting view of the economic scene, page 2. After listing a series of economic studies they go on to say:

"Conclusions of these sundry assessments did not always converge. Estimates of economic costs to timber-dependent communities and industries from implementing the ISC strategy ranged widely, from several thousand jobs to many tens of thousands of jobs. Many of these assessments did not deal with pecuniary or secondary effects (either costs or benefits). Most did not deal with positive aspects of changing economies, such as enhancements to secondary recreational industries, or the eventual hiring of hundreds of biologists and other resource specialists to inventory owls and study habitats and forestry effects. Rather, short-term, adverse effects on existing economic institutions seemed to be the prime interest and focus. And the outlook was typically painted as grim."

One must wonder how employment for more biologists and resource specialists helped the displaced timber worker.

The Marcot and Thomas report lists the "persistent, scientific questions.

"Among the questions not fully resolved are (1) What is the true, long-term demographic trend of the subspecies? (2) What is the relative contribution of this trend from management on Federal, State, private, and other forest lands? (3) What is the population response by owls under forest management objectives (e.g., to maintain long-term resource sustainability under Ecosystem Management) and new silvicultural approaches (e.g., small canopy-gap openings), particularly on Federal public lands? (4) What is the long-term effect of the continued invasion of the spotted owl's range by its prime avian competitor, the barred owl (*Strix varia*)? (5) How will the distribution and size of habitats called for in the new forest management plans specifically provide for interacting populations of spotted owls over time? (6) How will new fire and fuels management guidelines, and recent stand-replacing fire events, affect spotted owl populations, particularly in the drier or easterly portions of the Olympic Peninsula, Cascade Range, and interior northern California?" (Page 16) [354]

140

So, by late 1997 there were many questions still unanswered about the owl, even though it had been listed as threatened since1990.

A group of 50 scientists met in late 1998 to revisit owl data collected since a similar meeting in 1993. The press reports of that meeting[355] show that there may be some decline in the number of owls in some places, but there is no unequivocal evidence that the owl is about to go extinct.

A report of an independent research organization funded by the forest products industry sheds light on the owl situation. It reported on three hypotheses that had been tested. The first, that there was a tight link between owls and old growth abundance, showed that many other factors were also involved with owl abundance. For example, "In Washington, reproductive success for owls living in areas with extensive old-growth forests along the Cascade crest is 50 percent lower than for owls living in drier eastside forests that contain half as much late-successional and old-growth forests."

The second hypothesis, that northern spotted owls are experiencing an accelerating population decline across their geographic range, was being rejected. The researchers found that by using an improved model for owl populations that had fewer assumptions, it was not possible to demonstrate a decline in the survival rate of adult females. The third hypothesis, that forest fragmentation exacerbates the effects of habitat loss, also had to be rejected. In a research report published in a refereed journal, the scientists could not document that old forest distribution had such effects in western Oregon.[356]

Congress passed and President Clinton signed legislation that will provide to counties that have federal forestland in them direct payments in lieu of taxes.[357] Oregon is the state with the largest amount of land in that category. It is expected that these annual payments will amount to $13.4 million in Linn County, up from $8.0 million, and Benton County will received $3.6 million, up from $2.1 million. It remains to be seen, of course, what will happen at the end of the six years that this legislation specifies for the payments. That legislation is still in effect.

As President Clinton prepared to leave office in January 2001, he set aside some 60 million acres of federal land not previously set aside in wilderness and other reserved areas.[358] In 2002 President Bush is still delaying the implementation of the Clinton set-aside. It is not known what the production potential of federal forestland outside all the reserved areas is. It is not likely that the harvest will ever be even close the to 1989-1992 average of over five billion board feet shown above.

The spotted owl has served to halt timber harvest on much of the federal land in the Pacific Northwest. Harvest volume on the federal land in Oregon in 1997 was 0.67 billion board feet.[359] Harvest in 2002 is probably less than that.

The one nagging thought in this whole argument is the impact on people. We have seen a small sample of the letters that spelled out the pain and suffering that would come from the greatly reduced timber harvest on federal land in the region.

In 2000, the Cooperative Extension Service, Oregon State University, published a study on poverty in Oregon. It reported that the level of poverty in resource dependent communities was markedly higher than in the remainder of the state and attributed this condition to reduced timber harvest. Brief news stories appear all too often. Here is an example:

"Coos Bay worst in child abuse. COOS BAY. A decades-long run of bad economic luck, rampant methamphetamine use and old-fashioned ideas about how to run a family have given Coos Bay the worst child abuse rate in Oregon.

"Twenty-six percent of Coos County children live in poverty, compared with 16 percent statewide. The Coos County child abuse rate is 33.2 per 1,000 children, compared with 13.5 statewide.

"Last year, three children died and 473 were abused and neglected.

"Judy McMakin, director of the Coos County Commission on Children and Families, says agencies are working hard to counter the problem. *But the county has lost it sawmills, its fisheries—and in many cases, its best jobs* (emphasis added)."[360]

Michael Millstein reported in the *Oregonian* at the beginning of 2003 that, "More than half the 60,000 workers who held jobs in the wood products industry at the start of the 1990s had left it by 1998. And almost half of those who left disappeared from work rolls altogether – probably moving to another state, retiring or going unemployed."[361]

We will never know what could have been if the owl had not been listed. The economy of Oregon grew vigorously in the last decade of the 20th Century. There are those who feel it would not have happened if timber harvest had been permitted at a sustainable rate on federal land. There are those who feel that the Oregon's growth could have been even greater. The people whose livelihood and way of life was essentially destroyed in the timber dependent communities would be contributing to the economy rather than suffering. However, by the very nature of the human experience we will never know. We do know that Oregon in 2002 is suffering severe budgetary problems. A viable industry based on federal timber would surely be making that suffering less severe.

The condition and status of the agencies involved have changed. The U. S. Forest Service now must deal with all forest benefits without the money that came in from timber sales. The "Survey and Manage" language in the Northwest Forest Plan is such that no matter what the Forest Service attempts to meet the requirements of the Plan, someone can find fault and file a lawsuit that stops all activity in the area in question. The incumbent

Chief of the Forest Service is telling Congress that the Forest Service is paralyzed by analysis. The harvest levels on the national forests that were prescribed in the Northwest Forest Plan have yet to be met.

In 2002 a retired logging company president, Don Wimer, captured the magnitude of the changes that have occurred in the Northwest as a result of the listing of the NSO. He said, "It is unbelievable the changes that have occurred in this state (Oregon) since the owl was listed."

Forests have marvelous resiliency. So often we hear about fragile ecosystems. Fire, insects, wind, disease, floods and drought can seriously affect forests. Yet they recover. And so do the people that work in them. That resiliency of the people in the timber dependent communities is a thing just as beautiful as the forests, old and young, that surrounds them.

EPILOGUE

Studies of the biology of the northern spotted owl continue. I turned to a former colleague who has been involved with NSO research for over a decade and asked him for the latest on the owl. His responses, via Email, follow. From his comments it appears that models purporting to describe the population dynamics of the owl continue to show a decline. However, close scrutiny of the models, the forests, and the politics of science, leave one unsure of what the owls are really doing. It does seem that the owls are quite resourceful.

We have seen reports of Larry L. Irwin's work. He continues as a research biologist for The National Council of the Paper Industry for Air and Stream Improvement. Here are his responses to my inquiry about the owl's status in fall, 2001.

December 3, 2001—an Email from Dr. Irwin.

"The owl situation is complicated, so hold on: The 1993 report on owl population trends was published in Studies in Avian Biology in 1996.

"Results from the December 1998 workshop have not been published. There was some discussion about submitting the latest analyses to Wildlife Monographs, but apparently that won't happen. My recollection of the upshot of the latter workshop is that the owl population was considered to still be declining by some 3% per year or so (based upon the meta-analysis), but that several individual populations seemed to be holding relatively steady.

"Three sub-populations in NW California were considered to be declining at an accelerated rate, because they found that the "best" model accounting for variation in data was a linear trend in adult female survival rate for a log-linear model.

"In other field studies, we have been tracking over 100 adult owls with radio-transmitters for the past 3 years. So, we know for certain about their survival rates. Model-based estimates of owl adult survival at the last workshop ranged from 0.82-0.87 across the dozen or so owl-demography studies, while our empirical measure of survival for the past 3 years is several percentage points higher. If the model-based estimates, which are based upon re-observations of banded birds, are biased downward due to failure to meet crucial assumptions, a 2-3% upward adjustment in estimated survival rate would cause the investigators to change their conclusions.

"The crucial assumptions involve independent captures and independent survival rates, among males and females, and that adults do not emigrate. But we know that females are not captured unless their mated males are captured or re-observed first. And we know that adults may leave their territories (trend is for females to 'divorce' their mates and

144

move, sometime more than 20 miles). And given the sample sizes (ranging from 30-70 pairs or so), a 2-3% change would require only 1-3 birds per study area to move....

"That said, I must moderate a bit. Our own data, evaluated via the models and procedures used at the Dec. 98 workshop, suggested that the eastern Washington Cascades owl population may be declining at some 8% per year. While I don't believe the model-based estimates are so directly interpretable (violations of basic modeling assumptions mentioned above affect selection of a model to represent variation in the data, as well as subsequent interpretations), our empirical data attest to a decline in the number of pairs observed at nest sites, supporting a conclusion of a declining population for eastern Washington. Yet, correlations of reproductive success with estimates of vegetation and environmental conditions suggest that, if there is a decline, it is not related to forestry—there hasn't been any significant forestry for several years.

"What our data do suggest is that Douglas-fir dominated forests in the Grand Fir Zone are being invaded by grand fir trees, the climatic climax for intermediate-elevation forest zones. There, we found a negative correlation between small-diameter (13-20cm dbh) trees and owl reproduction; and there were more of such trees at sites that have apparently been abandoned. So, Douglas-firs are being replaced by grand fir, to the apparent detriment of spotted owls. Correlation does not equate to cause-and-effect, of course.

"But, advancing succession (and associated lack of forestry) is a reasonable explanation because Douglas-fir trees provide over 95% of the nesting sites (via broken-topped trees, mistletoe brooms, or nests abandoned by goshawks, which prefer Doug-firs too). The solution, of course, is reducing the densities of the trees: more forestry rather than less forestry.

"It gets worse. In that area, the most productive owls live in the Douglas-fir/ponderosa pine zone where there is not a large amount of old growth. The moist forests near the crest of the Cascades have the most old growth, but the owls there are not very productive. So, there is an influence of abiotic factors, and there are differences in owl performance among the several forest zones—no management plan has yet accounted for those very basic ecological differences. The really serious part is that the forests where the owls do best are at risk to devastating wildfires, owing to fire preclusion, advancing succession, and the associated insect and disease epidemic. I'm just about ready to submit a manuscript. from that work to Forest Ecology & Management. I believe that we'll get an even-handed review from that journal.

"We are also trying to secure funding for USFS (and Fire Plan) to conduct an adaptive management research experiment, in which thinnings are implemented within owl territories to reduce fuels, and also stimulate the owls via increasing energy flow to the owl's prey base, primarily via understory shrubs. We are also searching for verbal support as input to the PNW Station, to increase their awareness and interest.

Later, December 7, 2001:

"Hi Ben—I neglected to mention to you a recent paper on owl demography. It reports information from a single population in NW California, by Franklin et al. 2000, Ecolog. Monographs 70(4). It attracted The Wildlife Society's award for 'monograph of the year', and is indeed a good piece of work. I have a few problems with the paper: 1) the way the vegetation was classified; it was a dichotomous classification for analytical purposes—habitat was either considered suitable or unsuitable based upon pre-conceived notions. They did not allow for variation in stand structure. That, of course, reduced the number of parameters for modeling. 2) I do not trust model-based estimates of survival, primarily because the investigators did not account for failure to meet certain assumptions of capture-recapture theory. Female captures (and apparent survival), are not independent of captures of males. That doesn't change the point estimate of survival much, but does have the effect of changing the variance matrix to the extent that certain models are more likely to be identified as "good" models. 3) They did not have the ability to compare the responses of birds in white fir vs. Douglas-fir; their study was heavily weighted by birds in 49 sites in 1 small part of the area. So, in my opinion, the results cannot be extrapolated very far.

"Despite those criticisms, Franklin learned what some of us have been saying for a number of years: owls are not "interior-forest" species, owing to their exploitation of prey that use young successional stages, namely woodrats in Mixed Conifer forests and in that portion of their geographic range. There, the best habitat configuration involves mature and old forests interspersed with other vegetation types. Actually the "other" vegetation types are the brushy-stage clearcuts. They obviously had a difficult time saying that, because it would imply that forestry was benefiting the owls, so they labeled them as hardwood brush stands (I noted that because Franklin's dissertation uses different language). They were unable to distinguish among young and intermediate successional stages. Extensive late-seral Douglas-fir forest is detrimental to reproductive success, but helps adult survival. That can be predicted from current theory on biodiversity, which holds that the most productive zones are not the highest in diversity. Intermediate successional stages exhibit greater diversity of pathways of energy and nutrient flow; hence, more opportunities for a predator.

"Finally, they concluded that this particular population was stationary during the study period, that is, 'lambda" was around 1.0, despite a wide

146

range of variation in fitness of individual territories. Their previous conclusions for the same population from demographic analyses that supported listing the owl in 1990 was that the Willow Creek population was declining linearly, i.e., at an accelerating rate. In the 1993 demographic workshop, they concluded the population was declining slowly. They neglected to mention the changes in interpretations and why they may have been misled by the early analyses. I have a strong suspicion that happened because of the effects of non-independent captures of males and females: when a capture-recapture study on owls is concluded after a "good" nesting year for owls (years when more females are found), the estimates of lambda tend toward 1.0, or a stationary population. When a study concludes after a "poor" nesting year, as happened in the 1990 analysis that supported listing (based upon data through 1989) and in 1993, which led to the 1996 compendium, the tendency is to conclude a population is declining linearly. The latest analyses, which led to the most positive outlook for owls across their range, concluded following a relatively good nesting year (1998). One wonders why the latest analyses have not been published...

"Best regards, Larry"

So, one scientist ends with an ellipsis. Perhaps some day we will know enough of the complex biology of the northern spotted owl to be able to make rational decisions in natural resources management. At the beginning of the new millennium it is clear that we do not yet have that knowledge. To check this conclusion I called Eric Forsman and discussed the present state of owl research. My conversation with Dr. Forsman can be summarized thus:

> The overall trend in northern spotted owl population appears to be down, with much variation from one part of its range to another. For example, on BLM land near Roseburg, OR, the population appears to be stable. In the area on the east side of the Cascades, in Washington, the trend is down.

> Two factors may explain the overall trend. The original concern was over habitat, and that may still be a factor. The other factor is the invasion of the northern spotted owl habitat by the barred owl. The barred owl is dominating the sites where the two species interact; hence the northern spotted owl population in such places goes down as the barred owl population goes up.

So the tentative conclusion stands: we do not know enough about the complex forest system in which the owls operate. We do know, however, that the pain inflicted on the timber dependent communities has not subsided a decade and more following the listing of the northern spotted owl. The citations of the report on poverty by the Oregon State Extension Service and the Coos Bay article at the end of Chapter 15 attest to this.

The penultimate say in this long and painful story has to come from Liz VanLeeuwen. My recent (2002) conversations with her can be summarized thus:

The story of the northern spotted owl is a story full of human misery that need never have happened. My constituents in the old 37th District of Oregon knew there was no real problem with the owl. They had seen them in the trees around their homes on the edge of the forest on the east side of the Willamette Valley. They still do, and scientists like Dr. Irwin keep finding them in forests that are not old growth. The salt-of-the-earth people that lived and worked in the forests on my district were hurt terribly by the listing of the owl. Somehow we must find a way to factor in people in the Endangered Species Act and find a way to convince government scientists and bureaucrats to look at all the data. We can manage our natural resources in a way that serves the present and future generations of Oregonians. I believe that and will work tirelessly to have it happen.

As compiler of this history, I shall have the final word. I believe there are important lessons to be learned from the story of the spotted owl. They involve fundamentals of science, statistical methodology and the ways in which ideas interact with public policy.

The original hypothesis was that a closed link existed between old growth and owls—that northern spotted owls as a species could only persist in old growth forests.

This hypothesis was treated by many as proven fact and has had a dramatic impact on forest policy in the Pacific Northwest.

We know now that the owl is breeding successfully in forests that are not old growth. We do not know what the course of history would have been had forests other than roaded old growth been surveyed for owls. We do know that the owl's status, right or wrong, was used to halt most timber harvest on federal land in the Pacific Northwest (see Stahl's quote, Chap. Two)

Forests are dynamic, ever changing, systems. It is naïve to think that old growth stands can be maintained into perpetuity, with or without human intervention. Fire, wind, insects or disease inevitability take down the old trees and, thanks to succession and the dynamic nature of the system, the forests regrow. A blanket of old growth never existed in this region and it never will. The question society must ultimately answer is whether or not a substantial portion of the federal forests shall be used to produce wood products as well as other forest benefits.

The lessons we take from this history are important. If we are going to base public policy on science, we had better make real sure that the science is first rate. For example, the owl decline is based on models that have scarcely seen the light of day or are suspect (see the Russell Lande citations in Chapter 10). Science based statistical sampling assures that each sampling unit has an equal probability of being selected if the procedure is purely random. Had this happened with the early spotted owl sampling we would have had very different estimates of the population. Failure to do that is a fundamental flaw in the whole study, review and listing process for the owl. The history of science is replete with stories of faulty sampling and the misinformation that results. The spotted owl story only adds to the list of examples.

We keep hearing that we need to have more science-advised policy. Ultimately, outcomes will improve if and only if the science is rigorous and attempts to falsify null hypotheses are vigorous, the data collected comes from sampling that is well designed, and the scientists involved do their level best to leave their private biases on the doorstep. Colleges and universities are the institutions in our society charged with assuring that their graduates make that happen.

"Ideas make the world go around." That was a mantra of my major professor. And sometimes ideas make a mess, he should have added. The idea that old growth is sacred and that old trees should never be cut is very enticing. Tree sitters have given their lives in support of this idea. Part and parcel of the spotted owl controversy is a second idea, namely that there can never be enough old growth. Despite having millions of acres of old growth in Wilderness and other reserves, environmentalists insist that there is not enough old growth off limits to human management. President Clinton added millions of acres with his roadless area actions in the final days of his presidency.

The Pacific Northwest could be the wood basket of the world. Instead, the United States imports ever more wood from around the globe. The ecological hypocrisy of that policy flies in the face of common sense. How can we in good conscience continue to be the world's biggest consumers of wood products, while at the same time eliminating harvest of those products from our own national forests? Even in the northeast serious questions have been raised about preservation as contrasted with wise use. In an article titled, "The illusion of preservation: a global environmental argument for the local production of natural resources," three Harvard University faculty make a cogent case for the United States to use its own natural resources.[362]

How should the northern spotted owl have story evolved? The early studies could have looked at all forest environments where the owl lives. This would have raised some flags of concern. The people of the Pacific Northwest are unexcelled in finding solutions to concerns and problems. In forestry, the forest practice laws of Oregon, for example, are superb. We know how to manage forests to maintain productivity of all benefits. Because of the high productive potential of the forests of the region, we could have our cake and eat it too. We have the reserved areas, millions of acres of them. We could also be utilizing the wood being grown annually in areas outside the reserved areas. There would be family wage jobs, support for community infrastructure, and viable forests, streams, wildlife populations and scenic beauty. All of this with a sense of a job well done would raise to higher levels the sense of satisfaction that one sees in the face of one who says, "I'm an Oregonian."

ENDNOTES

[1] Gannett, Henry. 1902. <u>The Forests of Oregon</u>. USGS Professional Paper No. 4, Series H, Forestry, 1. Washington, DC. 36 pp.

[2] Andy Stahl. Symposium, Sixth Environmental Law Clinic, University of Oregon School of Law, Eugene, OR. March 5, 1988.

[3] Gutierrez, R. J. 1992. Natural History of the Northern Spotted Owl, In: Recovery Plan For Northern Spotted Owl—Draft. Chapter II. US Dept. of Interior. Washington, DC.

[4] Forsman, E. D. 1976. A preliminary investigation of the spotted owl in Oregon. M. S. thesis, Oregon State Univ., Corvallis, OR.

[5] _____. 1980. Habitat utilization by spotted owl in the western central Cascades of Oregon. Ph.D. thesis, Oregon State University, Corvallis, OR.

[6] _____, E.C Meslow, and H. M. Wright. 1984. Distribution and Biology of the spotted owl in Oregon. Wildlife Monographs 87:1-64.

[7] VanLeeuwen, Liz. 1986. Don't sacrifice jobs for spotted owls. Lebanon (OR) Express, Nov. 12, 1986.

[8] "Spotted owl decision will affect our future." 1986. Lebanon (OR) Express, Nov. 12, 1986.

[9] "Forced to choose: For birds or people?" 1986. Albany Democrat Herald, July 31, 1986.

[10] "Can have both" Letter to Democrat Herald, August 23, 1986.

[11] "Record of Decision Final Environmental Impact Statement on Management of Northern Spotted Owl in National Forests" 1992. USDA Forest Service, March 1992.

[12] Testimony of Rep. Liz VanLeeuwen, April 28, 1986. From her files.

[13] "Cutting Trees, Losing Forests." Editorial in Oregon Business. May 1986 issue.

[14] Jazz artist performs at protest. Albany Democrat Herald, May 27, 1986.

[15] Albany Democrat Herald, Aug. 8, 1986.

[16] Albany Democrat Herald, Aug. 13, 1986

[17] The New Era, Sweet Home, OR. Aug. 13, 1986.

[18] Ranger: Plan won't cut logging. 1986. Albany Democrat Herald, Nov. 14, 1986.

[19] Forest Service deluged by letters on spotted owl issue. 1986. Albany Democrat Herald, Nov. 11, 1986.

[20] Letter to regional forester, Nov. 5, 1986 from Rep. VanLeeuwen on House of Representatives letterhead.

[21] Hodel: Owls 'not an urgent problem'. Albany Democrat Herald Oct. 4, 1986.

[22] Memorandum from Dave Dietz and John McCulley on Oregon Resource Equity letterhead, 1270 Chemeketa St., NE, Salem, OR 97301. Nov. 3, 1986.

[23] Hatfield challenges FS over owls. Albany Democrat Herald, Oct. 24, 1986,

[24] WI hires PR firm to inform public about owl. Sweet Home The New Era. Oct. 22, 1986.

[25] A RESOLUTION IN OPPOSITION TO THE U. S. FOREST SERVICE'S PREFERRED ALTERNATIVE FORE MANAGEMENT OF THE NORTHERN SPOTTED OWL. Sweet Home Chamber of Commerce, Sweet Home, OR. Oct. 17, 1986.

[26] Owl politics. Christy Duncan, Sweet Home, OR. Albany Democrat Herald, Oct. 3, 1986.

[27] Judge blocks old-growth cut. Albany Democrat Herald, Sept. 27, 1986.

[28] Habitat Management For The Spotted Owl, Planning Report, Pacific Northwest Region, USDA—Forest Service, April 1987.

[29] Final Environmental Impact Statement on Management for the Northern Spotted Owl in the National Forests, Volumes I and II, USDA Forest Service, National Forest System, January 1992.

[30] Brown, Richard T., Congress to Blame for Overcutting. Resources Review, September 1987.

[31] Spotted Owls in Second-Growth Timber Ruled 'Surplus' by USFS. Bruce L. Engel. Counterpoint. Nov. 1987.

[32] The Northern Spotted Owl Status Review. U. S. Fish and Wildlife Service, Region 1, Portland, OR. Dec. 14, 1987.

[33] Ibid. 1.

[34] Ibid. 2, 3.

[35] Ibid. 3.a.

[36] Ibid. 4.

[37] Ibid. 7.

[38] Ibid. 3.

[39] Ibid. 12, 13.

[40] Schallau, C., D. Olson and W. Maki. 1988. An Investigation of Long-Term Impacts on the Economy of Oregon of Alternative Timber Supply Forecasts. Western Regional Science Assoc. Feb. 24-28, 1988.

[41] Company counts 25 mill closures in NW. Albany Democrat Herald Feb. 14, 1988.

[42] 'Let's Get a Rope'—The Public response to National Forest Planning. Counterpoint. April 1988.

[43] James Monteith, Executive Director, ONRC, 1161 Lincoln St., Eugene, OR 974001.

[44] Spotted owls not all in old growth. Albany Democrat Herald. March 26, 1988.

[45] Forest plan may change, speaker tells group here. Lebanon Express. April 20, 1988

[46] Audubon: Owls need old-growth. Albany Democrat Herald. May 6, 1988.

[47] Owl supporters sue for protection. Albany *Democrat Herald.* May 6, 1988.

[48] Court halts some timber sales. Albany *Democrat Herald.* May 19, 1988.

[49] County officials worried over impact of logging ban. Albany *Democrat Herald.* May 20, 1988.

[50] Leaked report: Owls' survival uncertain. Eugene *Register Guard,* April 5, 1988.

[51] Holding the preservationists accountable. Jim Petersen. Lebanon *Express.* June 1, 1988.

[52] Con H. Schallau. 1988. The Forest Products Industry and Community Stability: The Evolution of the Issue. Montana Business Quarterly, Summer 1988. Bur. Bus. and Econ. Res. Univ. Montana, Missoula.

[53] Cohen, Stephen S., and John Zyman. 1987. *Manufacturing matters: the myth of the post-industrial economy.* New York; Basic Books.

[54] Oregon Forest Fact Book. EVERGREEN Foundation. 1997.

[55] BLM warns owl fight will sharply reduce state's timber supply. Albany *Democrat Herald.* June 1, 1988.

[56] BLM finds 89 spiked trees in southern Oregon. Albany *Democrat Herald.* June 1, 1988.

[57] Tree spikings frustrating for both sides. Albany *Democrat Herald.* June 11, 1988.

[58] Court allows timber sales. Albany *Democrat Herald.* June 14, 1988.

[59] House votes to reduce federal timber sales. Albany *Democrat Herald.* June 9, 1988.

[60] Hatfield's blind spot. Forests lose protection. Editorial. Salem *Statesman Journal.* June 29, 1988.

[61] Mark Keiser: A timber faller talks about tree spikes. EVERGREEN Vol. 2, No. 7. July 1988

[62] Author says tree spiking valid tactic. Albany *Democrat Herald.* Nov. 1, 1988.

[63] Wylie Smith in *EVERGREEN,* Vol. 2, No. 3. 1988.

[64] Hatfield: Balance needed in old-growth logging fight. Albany *Democrat Herald.* Sept. 12, 1988.

[65] Task Force to seek a limit on acreage for spotted owl. Lebanon *Express.* Sept. 28, 1988

[66] James F. Torrence, Regional Forester, to Rep. Van Leeuwen, Sept. 28, 1988.

[67] George S. Dunlap, Asst. Secy., to Rep. Van Leeuwen, Oct. 27, 1988.

[68] Oregon's 1987 timber harvest: 8.2 billion bd. ft. *The New Era.* Oct. 5, 1988.

[69] Spotted owl can't survive, if trees cut, says speaker. Lebanon *Express.* Oct 19, 1988.

[70] Judge calls spotted owl decision "capricious" Albany *Democrat Herald* . Nov. 18, 1988.

[71] Logging protestors fined. Albany *Democrat Herald*. Nov. 10, 1988.

[72] BLM. Nov. 28, 1988.

[73] Editorial. Lebanon *Express*. Nov. 30, 1988.

[74] A lost forest. Letter to editor. Albany *Democrat Herald*. Dec. 1, 1988.

[75] Hatfield vows to restore cuts. Albany *Democrat Herald*. Dec. 1, 1988.

[76] Hatfield decries efforts to help the spotted owl. Albany *Democrat Herald*. Dec. 3, 1988.

[77] Save the loggers. *The New Era*. Dec. 7, 1988.

[78] Environmentalists criticize Hatfield. Albany *Democrat Herald*. Dec. 12, 1988.

[79] Owl habitat to receive protection. Albany *Democrat Herald*. Dec. 12, 1988.

[80] Environmentalists criticize federal plan to save spotted owl. Albany *Democrat Herald*. Dec. 13, 1988.

[81] Group's report warns of timber recession. Albany *Democrat Herald*. Dec. 20, 1988.

[82] Sweet Home mill plans expansion. Albany *Democrat Herald*. Dec. 20, 1988.

[83] ONRC goes on mass appeal rampage. Timber Topics, Douglas Timber Operators, Inc. Jan. 1989.

[84] ONRC Continues Frivolous Appeals. Timber Topics. Douglas Timber Operators, Inc. Feb. 1989.

[85] Letter to Gov. Neil Goldschmidt from Rep. Van Leeuwen. Dec. 29, 1988.

[86] Timber Wilderness Lock-up Irritates Legislator. Counterpoint. January 1989.

[87] The Biggest Issue. Robert L. Hill, Ed. Oregon Business Magazine. Jan. 1989.

[88] Spotted owls are studied again. Salem Statesman *Journal*. Feb. 2, 1989.

[89] Willamette National Forest Reviewing Comments. Forest Plan Newsletter. WNF. August 1988.

[90] Alternative J: Many Suggest Changes. Forest Plan Newsletter. WNF. January 1989.

[91] Preliminary data from MOM. Forest Plan Newsletter. WNF. June 1989.

[92] Statement of John Kunzman at a timber rally. Undated.

[93] No Compromise in Defense of Mother Earth. An interview with Dave Forman by Jerry Mason, Nov. 1988.

[94] Whisenhunt, John A. Letter to Editor of Sweet Home *The New Era*, Jan. 1, 1989.

[95] Oregon's Forest Resources. Con H. Schallau, Oregon Policy Choices. Bureau of Governmental Research and Service. University of Oregon. Eugene. 1989.

[96] Packwood: Ban Forest Appeals. Salem *Statesman-Journal*, January 16, 1989.

[97] Albany *Democrat Herald,* January 19\8, 1989.

[98] Lebanon *Express* January 18, 1989.

[99] Michael Donnelly, Salem *Statesman-Journal,* January 11, 1989.

[100] Editorial by Bruce Harris, Salem *Statesman-Journal,* January 19, 1989.

[101] Jerry Underwood, Albany *Democrat Herald,* January 19, 1989.

[102] Speaker is Optimistic about Timber. Lebanon *Express,* January 18, 1989.

[103] Editorial, Albany *Democrat Herald,* January 24, 1989.

[104] TIMBER/BUSINESS, *The New Era,* Sweet Home, OR January 25, 1989.

[105] Editorial in *EVERGREEN,* March/April, 1989. Evergreen Foundation. Grants Pass, OR.

[106] *EVERGREEN,* June 1998. 5000 Cirrus Dr., Suite 201, Medford, OR 97504. Vol. 9, No. 4.

[107] The Truth about our Ancient Forests, Troy Reinhart, *EVERGREEN,* March/April 1989,

[108] Larry Irwin. *EVERGREEN,* March/April 1989.

[109] Rashevsky, N. 1960. Mathematical Biophysics: Physico-Mathematical Foundations of Biology. Dover Publications. New York. Volumes I and II.

[110] Spotted owl RD & A program. US Forest Service, Regions 5 and 6. Hq. Portland Or.

[111] Spotted owls, Old Growth and the Economy of the Northwest. Northwest Forest Resource Council, 1500 SW First Ave., Suite 770, Portland, OR 97201. 67 pages, Page 66.

[112] Op. Cit. Pages 54 and 55.

[113] Op. Cit. Pages 59-64.

[114] Ethyl Iron: Two sides talk of old growth, spotted owls. Albany *Democrat Herald.* May 1, 1989.

[115] Spotted owl issue needs cooperation. Mike Kerrick, Eugene *Register Guard,* May 3, 1989.

[116] A bitter pill. Lebanon *Express,* May 3, 1989.

[117] Robert Heilman, Portland *The Oregonian,* May 3, 1989.

[118] The Portland *Oregonian,* May 3, 1989.

[119] Marian Nelson. Letter to Peter Jennings, ABC. Sweet Home *The New Era.* May 3, 1989.

[120] Spotted Owl RD&A Program. Regions 5 and 6, U. S. Forest Service, Portland, OR.

[121] Forest Service: Thinning could offset log shortage. Albany *Democrat Herald.* May 5, 1989.

[122] No catastrophe? It is if you are affected. Editorial, Albany *Democrat Herald,* May 6, 1989.

[123] Kathie Durbin, Portland *The Oregonian,* May 9, 1989.

[124] Laws are For Everyone. Letter to Sweet Home *The New Era,* May 10, 1989,

[125] Lisa Strycker, May 11. 1989, Eugene, *Register-Guard*, Eugene, OR.

[126] Sadler: timber shortage real issue in environmental wars. *The Capital Press*. May 12, 1989.

[127] Spotted owl summit tentatively set June 24. Albany *Democrat Herald*. May 12, 1989.

[128] Industry is threatened species. Sandra Schukar. Salem *Statesman Journal*, May 13, 1989.

[129] Owl and timber debate suffers from several misconceptions. Albany *Democrat Herald*, May 15, 1989.

[130] BLM: Timber cut will be a third less than average. Albany *Democrat Herald*, May 17, 1989.

[131] Save Children. Albany *Democrat Herald*. May 18, 1989.

[132] Federal Agencies Work on Owl Plan. Albany *Democrat Herald*. May 16, 1989.

[133] Timber Supply Related Facts Compiled by Rep. VanLeeuwen. May 15, 1989.

[134] Judge lifts ban on logging. Albany *Democrat Herald*. May 19, 1989.

[135] Sharing Nature. Albany *Democrat Herald*. May 19, 1989.

[136] Relocate owls. Albany *Democrat Herald*. May 10, 1989.

[137] Editor's mailbag. Albany *Democrat Herald*. May 22, 1989.

[138] Environmentalists file appeal over owl. Albany *Democrat Herald*. May 24, 1989.

[139] Owl options frustrate Northwest Lawmakers. Albany *Democrat Herald*. May 29, 1989.

[140] Hatfield: Forest furor hits homes, schools. Salem *Statesman Journal*. May 25, 1989.

[141] Packwood urges support for log export ban. Portland *The Oregonian*. May 24, 1989.

[142] There is still time to avert disaster. Albany *Democrat Herald*. May 31, 1989.

[143] Quarterly Journal, National Humane Education Society, 211 Gibson St., NW, Suite 104, Leesburg, VA 22075.

[144] Data on age classes on Detroit Ranger District provided to B. B. Stout in 1996 by the district office.

[145] How much is left? *Oregon Business*. June 1989.

[146] Activists vow to defend Earth. Albany *Democrat Herald*. June 3, 1989.

[147] Editorial: Timber remains 'basic' to Oregon. Albany *Democrat Herald*. June 1, 1989.

[148] 'New Forestry' seeks balance. Albany *Democrat Herald*. June 3, 1989.

[149] Portland *The Oregonian*. June 4, 1989.

[150] Reaction mixed to forest agenda. The Eugene *Register Guard*. June 14, 1989.

[151] Public officials responsible for Northwest timber policy. Portland *The Oregonian*. June 5, 1989.

[152] Environmentalists seek more representation at summit. Albany *Democrat Herald*. June 8, 1989.

[153] It's time to speak out on timber issue. Eugene *Register Guard*. June 12, 1989.

[154] Environmentalists see ample timber. Portland *The Oregonian*. June 10, 1989.

[155] Rangers count old trees, owls. Albany *Democrat Herald*. June 10, 1989.

[156] Rep. Outlines timber concerns to new Speaker of House. Sweet Home *The New Era*. June 14, 1989.

[157] Owl spotted near timber sale. Albany *Democrat Herald*. June 15, 1989.

[158] Forest Service, O & C boost Linn forecasts. Albany *Democrat Herald*. June 16, 1989.

[159] Timber groups say logs to last through summer. Albany *Democrat Herald*. June 6, 1989.

[160] Ex-forester: Crisis could have been avoided. Albany *Democrat Herald*. June 17, 1989.

[161] Capitol Hill fights over spotted owl. Albany *Democrat Herald*. June 20, 1989.

[162] Timber harvest proposed. Eugene *The Register Guard*. June 21, 1989.

[163] 2 Northwest congressmen block bid to reduce old-growth timber harvests. *The Oregonian*. June 21, 1989.

[164] Congressmen call old growth a national issue. Albany *Democrat Herald*. June 21, 1989.

[165] Public split on timber issues. Albany *Democrat Herald*. June 22, 1989.

[166] Environmentalists have advantage, senator says. Albany *Democrat Herald*. June 23, 1989.

[167] Spikes found in logs. Albany *Democrat Herald*. June 23, 1989.

[168] Federal Register. Vol. 54, No 120, June 23, 1989. Pp 26666-26677.

[169] Timber compromise: Will it fly? Albany *Democrat Herald*. June 26, 1989.

[170] Plan offers old-growth breathing room. Op-Ed by Phil Cogswell. Portland *The Oregonian*. June 27, 1989.

[171] Environmentalists say no to deal. Albany *Democrat Herald*. June 27, 1989.

[172] Election: Loud 'no' to log exports. Albany *Democrat Herald*. June 28, 1989.

[173] Owl talks collapse again. Albany *Democrat Herald*. June 29, 1989.

[174] Agency chief: Owl data too skimpy. Albany *Democrat Herald*. June 23, 1989.

[175] Hatfield criticizes appeals court. Albany *Democrat Herald*. July 1, 1989.

[176] EVERGREEN. July/August 1989.

[177] Mark A Stein. Los Angeles *Times*. July 14, 1989

[178] Rep. Hayden asks full review before listing owl. *The New Era*. July 3, 1989.

[179] Owl family researched in Library of Congress. Lebanon *Express*. July 5, 1989.

[180] Forum. Lebanon *Express*. July 5, 1989.

[181] Oregon Project hands out dollar dots. Lebanon *Express*. July 5, 1989.

[182] Take time to think. Lebanon *Express*. July 5, 1989.

[183] Vandalism halts work at logging site. Albany *Democrat Herald*. July 6, 1989.

[184] Protesters block Siskiyou forest logging. Albany *Democrat Herald*. July 11, 1989.

[185] Environmentalists blamed in layoffs *and* Oregon senator says owl talks to continue. Albany *Democrat Herald*. July 7, 1989.

[186] Timber bids soar due to shortage. Albany *Democrat Herald*. July 7, 1989.

[187] Environmentalists plan to present counter-offer. Albany *Democrat Herald*. July 8, 1989.

[188]Group hopes to invite visitors for close look at timber families. Albany *Democrat Herald*. July 8, 1989.

[189] Rep. DeFazio talks timber policy. Lebanon *Express*. July 12, 1989.

[190] Owl lawsuit: Goldschmidt plans to file brief. Albany *Democrat Herald*. July 14, 1989.

[191] Latest plan for forests rejected by industry. Albany *Democrat Herald*. July 18, 1989.

[192] Lawmakers meet over logging *and* Timber company to leave buffer for owl. Albany *Democrat Herald*. July 19, 1989.

[193] Reducing timber cut could devastate Oregon Labor Press. July 19, 1989.

[194] Owl explosion. Albany *Democrat Herald*. July 21, 1989.

[195] Lawmakers offer compromise plan in fight over owl. Albany *Democrat Herald*. July 24, 1989.

[196] Senate panel Oks Hatfield-Adams timber compromise. Albany *Democrat Herald*. July 25, 1989.

[197] Senate passes temporary truce in timber fight. Albany *Democrat Herald*. July 27, 1989.

[198] Timber supports latest proposal. Lebanon *Express*. July 26, 1989.

[199] Timber dispute turns to national struggle. Albany *Democrat Herald*. July 28, 1989.

[200] Owl lawyer investigated. Albany *Democrat Herald*. July 31, 1989.

[201] Letter to Marvin Plenert, USFWS. From John Kunzman, July 31, 1989.

[202] Timber related supply facts, August 1989. Information letter on Rep. VanLeeuwen's House of Rep. letterhead.

[203] Chadsey, Phillip D. 1989. Is the Owl Really Threatened? Oregon Business, August 1989, page 54, 56, 57.

[204] Packwood proposes new rules for appeals of forest decisions. Albany *Democrat Herald.* August 1, 1989.

[205] Decision on timber plan delayed. Eugene *Register-Guard.* August 2, 1989.

[206] Lebanon FISH funds dwindling. Albany *Democrat Herald.* August 4, 1989.

[206] Demonstrators protest road building near owl. *The Oregonian.* August 6, 1989.

[207] Agency chief; Owl rules too restrictive. Albany *Democrat Herald.* August 5, 1989.

[208] Demonstrators protest road building near owl. *The Oregonian.* August 6, 1989.

[209] Timber industry backing Oregon's political power. Eugene *Register-Guard.* August 6, 1989.

[210] Timber sale planning continues despite spotted owl injunctions. Sweet Home *The New Era.* August 9, 1989.

[211] Yellow Ribbon Express, Communities for a Greater Oregon, Sweet Home, OR August 10, 1989.

[212] Spotted owl hearings to begin. Albany *Democrat Herald.* August 12, 1989.

[213] Letter to President George Bush, August 11, 1989, from Rep. VanLeeuwen.

[214] Letter to Lacy Logan, Stroh Brewing Co., Detroit, MI. from Rep. Van Leeuwen, August 11, 1989.

[215] Letter to Senator Hatfield from Rep. VanLeeuwen, August 11, 1989.

[216] Testimony by Dr. Hal Salwasser, Deputy Director Wildlife and Fisheries, USDA Forest Service, at a field hearing held by USFWS in Portland, OR August 14, 1989.

[217] Timber interests plan public relations blitz. Albany *Democrat Herald.* August 14, 1989.

[218] Activists climb trees to launch protests. Albany *Democrat Herald.* August 14, 1989.

[219] Memorandum to constituents re: spotted owl listing. Rep. VanLeeuwen. August 14, 1989.

[220] Limits on logging debated. Eugene *Register-Guard.* August 15, 1989.

[221] Hearing told owl numbers greater. Eugene *Register Guard.* August 18, 1989.

[222] TIMBER, by Timber Resource Education, Inc. Creswell, OR. Vol. 3, Issue 8. August 1989.

[223] BETA Funds Available. Corvallis *Gazette Times.* August 23, 1989

[224] Spotted owl issue cuts timber sales in Coos Bay. Albany *Democrat Herald.* August 26, 1989.

[225] Conservationists told to plan for all forests. Albany *Democrat Herald.* August 28, 1989.

[226] Owl decision to beat deadline. Eugene *Register-Guard.* August 29, 1989.

[227] Log truck gets mighty send off. Sweet Home *New Era.* August 30, 1989.

[228] Packwood: Forest Service hurt chances of timber bill. Albany *Democrat Herald.* August 31, 1989.

[229] Letter to Rep. Sidney Yates, US House of Rep. from Rep. VanLeeuwen. August 31, 1989.

[230] Oregon timber delegation heading to Washington. Albany *Democrat Herald.* September 4, 1989.

[231] Court lifts old growth injunction. Albany *Democrat Herald.* September 6, 1989.

[232] Lifting owl injunction won't free all timber. Albany *Democrat Herald.* September 7, 1989.

[233] Unions rally for timber legislation. Eugene *Register-Guard.* September 9, 1989.

[234] Who needs old growth? In Oregon we all do. Albany *Democrat Herald.* September 13, 1989.

[235] Union rally fizzles. Sweet Home *The New Era.* September 13, 1989.

[236] Logging showdown this week? Eugene *Register-Guard.* September 11, 1989.

[237] Old-growth showdown could come this week. Albany *Democrat Herald.* September 11, 1989.

[238] Drunk or sober. Albany *Democrat Herald.* September 18, 1989.

[239] Lobbying over timber intensifies. Eugene *Register-Guard.* September 12, 1989.

[240] Key lawmakers meet on spotted owl issue. Albany *Democrat Herald.* September 21, 1989.

[241] Panel member rejects new old-growth plan. Albany *Democrat Herald.* September 26, 1989.

[242] Panel gets old-growth compromise. Albany *Democrat Herald.* September 29, 1989.

[243] Both sides agree spotted owl pact 'too little too late.' Albany *Democrat Herald.* September 30, 1989.

[244] If timber supply holds, western lumber outlook good. Sweet Home *The New Era.* September 20, 1989

[245] Wilderness Society: Charge for forest use. Albany *Democrat Herald.* September 29, 1989.

[246] Study: Restriction of wilderness OK. Albany *Democrat Herald.* September 5, 1989.

[247] TBS: Network will stand by show. Albany *Democrat Herald.* September 26, 1989.

[248] Local Oregon Project mulls CGO merger. Lebanon *Express*. September 27, 1989.

[249] The spotted owl fiasco. Sweet Home *The New Era*. September 20, 1989.

[250] Environmentalists seek halt to logging. Albany *Democrat Herald*. September 14, 1989.

[251] ONRC winds appeal, timber sale stopped. *Capital Press*. September 23, 1988.

[252] Eco-Kamikazes Wanted. Earth First! Journal. September 22, 1989.

[253] Ranger district to sell timber. Albany *Democrat Herald*. November 10, 1989.

[254] Protests filed against timber sales. Albany *Democrat Herald*. October 7, 1989.

[255] Environmentalists challenge 'truce.' Albany *Democrat Herald*. October 27, 1989.

[256] Speaker: Owls can survive logging. Albany *Democrat Herald*. October 13, 1989.

[257] Policy could protect over half of old-growth. Albany *Democrat Herald*. October 20, 1989.

[258] Preservationists give example of treachery. Lebanon *Express*. November 1, 1989.

[259] Viewpoint. *Daily Journal of Commerce*. November 6, 1989.

[260] Judge says timber harvest can proceed. Albany *Democrat Herald*. November 7, 1989.

[261] BLM wants owl lawsuit dismissed. Albany *Democrat Herald*. November 19, 1989.

[262] Linn tops timber-study list. Albany *Democrat Herald*. November 6, 1989.

[263] Oregon Fish and Wildlife Journal. Fall, 1989.

[264] The Law and the Public Will. From Evergreen Magazine. Sweet Home *The New Era*. November 15, 1989.

[265] District Ranger talks to Third Force. Lebanon *Express*. November 22, 1989.

[266] OSU suggests timber cuts to sustain future harvests. *Capital Press*. November 24, 1989.

[267] Albany timber industry rep named to advisory board. Albany *Democrat Herald*. November 24, 1989.

[268] Counties asked to help pay costs of fight over owl. Albany *Democrat Herald*. November 25, 1989.

[269] User fees proposed. *Evergreen* November, 1989.

[270] OSU researches spotted owl, habitat. Lebanon *Express*. November 22, 1989.

[271] Letter to editors. Liz VanLeeuwen, December 5, 1989.

[272] Study finds 36 spotted owls in SH district. Albany *Democrat Herald*. December 6, 1989.

[273] Timber support group plans meeting. Albany *Democrat Herald*. December 6, 1989.

[274] Oregon's Not-So-Sweet Home. NEWSWEEK. December 12, 1989.

[275] S. H. Chamber President Responds to Newsweek. Sweet Home *The New Era*. December 13, 1989.

[276] Letter from James E. Brown to Regional Director, USFWS. December 15, 1989.

[277] Willamette hits record in log bid. Albany *Democrat Herald*. December 19, 1989.

[278] Willamette Forest leads nation. Albany *Democrat Herald*. December 19, 1989.

[279] Opposite views are last word on owls. Albany *Democrat Herald*. December 20, 1989,

[280] Firms continue high timber bids. Albany *Democrat Herald*. December 20, 1989.

[281] Group's report warns of timber recession. Albany *Democrat Herald*. December 20, 1989,

[282] Resources council challenges sales in 4 BLM districts. Albany *Democrat Herald*. December 27, 1989.

[283] Lead quotation in a four-page Oregon Natural Resources Council recruitment mailing. Estimated to have been mailed in either late 1989 or early 1990.

[284] Letter to F. Dale Robertson, Chief, U. S. Forest Service from Liz Van Leeuwen, February 16, 1990.

[285] New Revised Oregon Forest Fact Book. 1997. Published by Evergreen Foundation, 5000 Cirrus Drive, Suite 201, Medford, OR 97504.

[286] Is The Northern Spotted Owl Really Threatened? Brochure, undated, by Northwest Forest Resource Council, 1500 S. W. First Ave., Suite 770, Portland, OR 97201.

[287] Simpson plans owl study. Albany *Democrat Herald*. January 8, 1990.

[288] Warren Brooks. April 1, 1990. *Washington Times*, Washington, D. C.

[289] Forest Watch. *The New Era*. January 17, 1990.

[290] Environmentalists question memos. Albany *Democrat Herald*. January 18, 1990.

[291] Advisory panel takes on large task. Albany *Democrat Herald*. January 18, 1990.

[292] Letter to John Hart, *Christian Science Monitor*, Boston, MA. January 22, 1990, from Rep. Liz VanLeeuwen.

[293] Environmentalists vow tougher fight. Albany *Democrat Herald*. January 24, 1990.

[294] Ranger District-City: Economic Partnership? *The New Era*. January 24, 1990.

[295] Hit by nature. Letter to Editor by Karen Clark, Idanha, OR. Albany *Democrat Herald.* January 25, 1990.

[296] Panel member says he's optimistic about timber compromise, and, Members of Eugene panel call timber boards "a sham." Albany *Democrat Herald.* January 25, 1990.

[297] BLM renews request to cut dead timber in owl areas. Albany *Democrat Herald.* January 31, 1990.

[298] BLM district drops salvage of dead timber in owl zone. Albany *Democrat Herald.* February 9, 1990.

[299] Letter to Rep. VanLeeuwen from Karen Barnette, District Ranger, Sweet Home Ranger District. Feb. 13, 1990.

[300] Letter from VanLeeuwen to F. Dale Robertson, Chief of Forest Service, on House of Representatives letterhead, dated February 16, 1990.

[301] *EVERGREEN,* February 1990.

[302] BLM timber sales rejected to save owl. Eugene *Register Guard.* March 10, 1990.

[303] Officials to review owl study. Albany *Democrat Herald.* March 12, 1990,

[304] Lawmakers worried about timber fate. Albany *Democrat Herald.* March 12, 1990.

[305] Letter to VanLeeuwen from Robert F. Smith, U. S. House of Representatives. March 12, 1990.

[306] Letter from Rep. VanLeeuwen to constituents. March 20, 1990.

[307] Albany *Democrat Herald,* April 3, 1990.

[308] Albany *Democrat Herald.* April 4, 1990.

[309] Albany *Democrat Herald.* April 5, 1990.

[310] Owls prefer forest that looks a mess. Albany *Democrat Herald.* April 6, 1990.

[311] Thousands rally to protect timber jobs. Eugene *Register Guard.* April 14, 1990.

[312] A Job Well Done. Sweet Home *The New Era.* April 18, 1990.

[313] What's the purpose of national forests? Albany *Democrat Herald.* April 23, 1990.

[314] Three mills closing down in mid-valley. Albany *Democrat Herald.* April 27, 1990.

[315] Albany *Democrat Herald* May 2, 1990.

[316] Lebanon *Express.* May 2, 1990.

[317] U. S. Report: Plan to save owl carries big price tag. Eugene *Register Guard.* May 4, 1990.

[318] Poll shows Oregonians deeply split over owl. Portland *Sunday Oregonian.* May 6, 1990.

[319] The Portland *Oregonian.* May 17, 1990.

[320] The Eugene *Register Guard.* May 20, 1990.

[321] The Albany *Democrat Herald.* May 28, 1990.

[322] Agency will avoid sales in proposed owl areas. Albany *Democrat Herald.* June 5, 1990.

[323] Wildlife agency will have final say of timber cuts. Albany *Democrat Herald.* June 23, 1990.

[324] Biologist: Owl study was once 'a lot of fun.' Albany *Democrat Herald.* June 23, 1990.

[325] Congressmen: Impact unknown. Albany *Democrat Herald.* June 23, 1990.

[326] Governor: Prevent 'devastation.' Albany *Democrat Herald.* June 23, 1990.

[327] Science alone must not dictate. Albany *Democrat Herald.* June 23, 1990.

[328] Letter to W. E. Sinclair from Mark O. Hatfield, May 7, 1990.

[329] AuCoin: Owl will have impact on private lands. Albany *Democrat Herald.* April 3, 1990.

[330] AG's owl response looks too legalistic. Albany *Democrat Herald.* April 11, 1990.

[331] Owl plan means economic chaos, lawmakers say. Albany *Democrat Herald.* May 4, 1990.

[332] AuCoin: Plan could trigger a recession. Albany *Democrat Herald.* May 8, 1990.

[333] Job losses may be worse than predicted, Smith says. Albany *Democrat Herald.* May 11, 1990.

[334] Bush cites `human equation' in debate over spotted owl. The Portland *Oregonian.* May 21, 1990.

[335] Letter to President Bush from Liz VanLeeuwen. May 20, 1990, with enclosures.

[336] Governor sees threat to economy. The Eugene *Register-Guard.* June 24, 1990.

[337] Groups: 65 percent of sales of timber violate owl pact. Albany *Democrat Herald.* April 3, 1990.

[338] Environmentalist: 4 million acres will be set aside for owl. Albany *Democrat Herald. April 4, 1990.*

[339] A conservation strategy for the northern spotted owl. Interagency Scientific Committee. Jack Ward Thomas, Chairman. Portland, OR April 2, 1990.

[340] ONRC solicitation letter very revealing. Lebanon *Express.* April 18, 1990.

[341] Environmental leaders get paid big bucks. Lebanon *Express.* June 13, 1990.

[342] Environmentalists get their turn with national advisers. Albany *Democrat Herald.* June 16, 1990.

[343] President George Bush from Kevin R. Williams. April 5, 1990.

[344] Letter to editor, Lebanon *Express.* April 18, 1990, from Patrick Tomlin.

[345] Open letter: Re: Northern Spotted owl. April 18, 1990. Gene Hansen, Corvallis, OR.

[346] Letter to Rep. VanLeeuwen from Clifford Ellis Worthylake, Mapleton, OR. April 26, 1990.

[347] Letter to Rep. VanLeeuwen, June 12, 1990. Mr. and Mrs. Dan Usher, Lebanon, OR.

[348] Costly `science' Albany *Democrat Herald.* June 2, 1990.

[349] Clinton to ban road building in forests. Albany *Democrat Herald.* January 4, 2001.

[350] Thomas defends owl plan. Albany *Democrat Herald.* July 19, 1990.

[351] Prof says timber losses can be offset. Albany *Democrat Herald.* July 19, 1990.

[352] Letter to Honorable Liz VanLeeuwen from Manuel Lujan. July 24, 1990.

[353] Employment Data. From Rep. Liz VanLeeuwen. March 20, 1992.

[354] Of Spotted Owls, Old Growth and New Policies: A History Since the Interagency Scientific Report. September 1997. Gen. Tech. Report. PNW-GTR-408.

[355] Spotted owl health trends still fuzzy report says. *Capital Press.* July 30, 1999.

[356] Forestry Environmental Program News. NCASI. Vol 11, No. 8, Aug. 4, 1999.

[357] Forest aid bill will benefit Linn, Benton. Albany *Democrat Herald. Oct. 11, 2000.*

[358] Clinton to ban road building in forests. Albany *Democrat Herald.* January 5, 2001.

[359] Forest Fact Book, 1999 Edition. The Oregon Forest Resources Institute. 808 SW Third Ave., Portland, OR 97204.

[360] Coos Bay worst in child abuse. Salem *Statesman Journal.* December 12, 2000.

[361] Loggers displaced in 1990s left behind, study finds. Portland *Oregonian.* January 7, 2003.

[362] Berlick, M. M., D. B. Kittredge and D. R. Foster. 2002. The illusion of preservation: a global environmental argument for the local production of natural resources. Journal of Biogeography. Vol. 29, Numbers 10/11, October/November 2002. pages 1557-1568.

INDEX

www.ingramcontent.com/pod-product-compliance
Lightning Source LLC
Chambersburg PA
CBHW020507290526
45786CB00002B/510